Contents

access to history

LABOUR *and* REFORM: WORKING-CLASS MOVEMENTS 1815–1914

Second Edition

Clive Behagg

Hodder & Stoughton

A MEMBER OF THE HODDER HEADLINE GROUP

Acknowledgements
The front cover shows JK Hardie by S Pankhurst, reproduced courtesy of the National Portrait Gallery, London.

The publishers would like to thank the following individuals, institutions and companies for permission to reproduce copyright illustrations in this book:
The British Library Newspaper Library page 32; Katz Pictures Ltd page 41; The Illustrated London News Picture Library page 63; Punch page 78; The Ironbridge Gorge Museum Trust page 86; Will Dyson/Daily Herald 3 December 1913/Centre for the Study of Cartoon and Caricature, University of Kent, Canterbury page 131; The British Library Newspaper Library page 136.

The publishers would also like to thank the following for permission to reproduce material in this book:
Hamlyn for the extract from *Fifty Years March* by Francis William, Odhams Press, 1949; ITPS Ltd for the extract from *Popular Politics in Nineteenth Century England*, Routledge, 1998; McGill-Queen's University Press for the extract from *Thomas Atwood: The Biography of a Radical*, 1990.

Every effort has been made to trace and acknowledge ownership of copyright. The publishers will be glad to make suitable arrangements with any copyright holders whom it has not been possible to contact.

Orders: please contact Bookpoint Ltd, 78 Milton Park, Abingdon, Oxon OX14 4TD. Telephone (44) 01235 827720, Fax: (44) 01235 400454. Lines are open from 9.00–6.00, Monday to Saturday, with a 24-hour message answering service. Email address: orders@bookpoint.co.uk

British Library Cataloguing in Publication Data
A catalogue record for this title is available from the British Library

ISBN 0 340 75809 0

First published 1991
Impression number   10 9 8 7 6 5 4 3 2 1
Year   2005 2004 2003 2002 2001 2000

Typeset by Fakenham Photosetting Limited, Fakenham, Norfolk.
Printed in Great Britain for Hodder & Stoughton Educational, a division of Hodder Headline Plc, 338 Euston Road, London NW1 3BH by Redwood Books Ltd, Trowbridge, Wilts.

Preface

To the general reader

Although the *Access to History* series has been designed with the needs of students studying the subject at higher examination levels very much in mind, it also has a great deal to offer the general reader. The main body of the text (i.e. ignoring the 'Study Guides' at the ends of chapters) forms a readable and yet stimulating survey of a coherent topic as studied by historians. However, each author's aim has not merely been to provide a clear explanation of what happened in the past (to interest and inform): it has also been assumed that most readers wish to be stimulated into thinking further about the topic and to form opinions of their own about the significance of the events that are described and discussed (to be challenged). Thus, although no prior knowledge of the topic is expected on the reader's part, she or he is treated as an intelligent and thinking person throughout. The author tends to share ideas and possibilities with the reader, rather than passing on numbers of so-called 'historical truths'.

To the student reader

Although advantage has been taken of the publication of a second edition to ensure the results of recent research are reflected in the text, the main alteration from the first edition is the inclusion of new features, and the modification of existing ones, aimed at assisting you in your study of the topic at AS level, A level and Higher. Two features are designed to assist you during your first reading of a chapter. The *Points to Consider* section following each chapter title is intended to focus your attention on the main theme(s) of the chapter, and the issues box following most section headings alerts you to the question or questions to be dealt with in the section. The *Working on...* section at the end of each chapter suggests ways of gaining maximum benefit from the chapter.

There are many ways in which the series can be used by students studying History at a higher level. It will, therefore, be worthwhile thinking about your own study strategy before you start your work on this book. Obviously, your strategy will vary depending on the aim you have in mind, and the time for study that is available to you.

If, for example, you want to acquire a general overview of the topic in the shortest possible time, the following approach will probably be the most effective:

1. Read Chapter 1. As you do so, keep in mind the issues raised in the *Points to Consider* section.
2. Read the *Points to Consider* section at the beginning of Chapter 2 and decide whether it is necessary for you to read this chapter.
3. If it is, read the chapter, stopping at each heading or sub-heading to note

down the main points that have been made. Often, the best way of doing this is to answer the question(s) posed in the Key Issues boxes.

4. Repeat stage 2 (and stage 3 where appropriate) for all the other chapters.

If, however, your aim is to gain a thorough grasp of the topic, taking however much time is necessary to do so, you may benefit from carrying out the same procedure with each chapter, as follows:

1. Try to read the chapter in one sitting. As you do this, bear in mind any advice given in the *Points to Consider* section.

2. Study the flow diagram at the end of the chapter, ensuring that you understand the general 'shape' of what you have just read.

3. Read the *Working on...* section and decide what further work you need to do on the chapter. In particularly important sections of the book, this is likely to involve reading the chapter a second time and stopping at each heading and sub-heading to think about (and probably to write a summary of) what you have just read.

4. Attempt the *Source-based questions* section. It will sometimes be sufficient to think through your answers, but additional understanding will often be gained by forcing yourself to write them down.

When you have finished the main chapters of the book, study the 'Further Reading' section and decide what additional reading (if any) you will do on the topic.

This book has been designed to help make your studies both enjoyable and successful. If you can think of ways in which this could have been done more effectively, please contact us. In the meantime, we hope that you will gain greatly from your study of History.

Keith Randell & Robert Pearce

1 Introduction: Labour and Reform 1815–1914

POINTS TO CONSIDER

In order to understand working-class movements, and the way they developed from 1815 to 1914, it is important to place them into the context of the time in which they happened. This will involve you in relating these movements to the social and economic changes taking place as Britain industrialised. Even more difficult, you will need to try to see these movements as they would have been seen by their participants at the time. This is complicated for us by the fact that many of the first and most influential historians of radical movements writing in the early twentieth century (like G.D.H. Cole. the Hammonds, and the Webbs) were themselves participants in the infant Labour Party. They were therefore inclined to see, for example, the Chartists as the forerunners of the Labour Party. Of course, the Chartists could not have known how the story was to turn out. So, our history is complicated by the fact that before our period was complete the historical analysis of it had begun.

1 Labour's Long Road to Citizenship

KEY ISSUE How can we, as historians, come to understand nineteenth-century working-class movements in their own terms?

The metaphor most often used to describe the development of working-class movements in the nineteenth and early twentieth centuries is that of a journey or, more evocatively, a 'march'. The journey runs from a point around 1815, where workers find themselves without the means to defend their way of life, possessing neither the vote nor the right to form trade unions. They travel slowly and with many setbacks to a point in the early twentieth century when, having achieved both the vote and legal status for their unions, working people become full political members of a mature industrial nation, a situation exemplified in the growing strength of the newly formed Labour Party.

The image of labour's 'long march' to citizenship can be very helpful in trying to understand the continuities in the evolution of working-class movements, but it can also be confusing. It is easy, for example, to assume that our travellers were aware of their ultimate destination from the start or that if they were not this was due to some fault on their part. Groups like the Chartists who campaigned for full voting rights for working-class men in the first half of the nineteenth century are sometimes seen as being premature in their demands, 'ahead of their time', or simply impatient hotheads unwilling to await the gradual unfolding of the democratic process. The wisest of the reformers seem, from this perspective, to be those who recognised that such changes could not be achieved in the twinkling of an eye. Yet to understand early nineteenth-century working-class movements fully we must appreciate the widespread desire for immediate and comprehensive change, and the bitter disappointment when this was not achieved. We know how the journey ended and, with the benefit of hindsight, we can see that change would come about in the fullness of time, but this is not how it appeared at the time.

This view from the present time has sometimes tended to distort our full understanding of the way working-class movements developed. It carries with it the implicit assumption that it was 'inevitable' that things would work out in the way that they did; that change would come gradually and by agreement, rather than suddenly and by revolutionary force. The gradualness of change is sometimes felt to reflect a rather elusive entity called 'the British character', which is supposed to be supremely cautious and eminently reasonable. The fact that these sorts of changes occurred more violently elsewhere (notably France) has often been seen to confirm British views on the unpredictable volatility of foreigners in general (and the French in particular). Yet this rather complacent approach deflects the historian from a full consideration of the way these movements actually looked to the people who were involved at the time.

Instead of reading history back from the present in this rather mechanical fashion, this book approaches the topic of working-class movements in the years 1815 to 1914, with two assumptions in mind. First, that these movements represented responses by working people to the process of change. In order to understand the way these responses were fashioned the historian must appreciate the view of the world that was held by the participants of these movements.

Secondly, it is assumed in the following chapters that the responses from within the working community changed as the context from which it grew altered. In this period society was undergoing industrialisation and urbanisation and as these two processes took effect they influenced the nature of working-class movements. Thus, for example, trade unionism in the period up to 1850 differed significantly from the exclusive 'new model' unions of highly skilled workers that developed in the 1850s and 1860s. Similarly, the swing towards union organisation among the less skilled members of the workforce in the years after 1885 reflected the fact that Britain's role in the world economy was shifting significantly at this time. What all this means is that, in order to understand the nature of any popular movement, the historian must place it fully in the complex economic and social context of its time, because the movement under scrutiny was a response to that context.

2 The Changing Context 1815–1914

> **KEY ISSUE** What is the relationship between working-class movements and the social and economic changes associated with the Industrial Revolution?

The years 1815 to 1914 took British society from the end of one major European war to the start of another. The main determinant of change in this period was the process of industrialisation. The impact of this was so all pervading that historians in the 1880s, looking back on the recent past, felt that British society had undergone a revolution. It was at this time that the term 'Industrial Revolution' was coined as a way of expressing the changes that the late-Victorians recognised as having occurred within living memory.

The extent of these changes might be summarised in the following way. In 1815 the United Kingdom was a predominantly agricultural nation and most of its population of just over 19 million people lived in the countryside. It was dominated politically by a landed aristocracy and less than 5 per cent of the adult population (men and women) were entitled to vote in parliamentary elections. By 1914 the United Kingdom was an industrial nation with a population of 46 million people who lived mostly in the towns. The basis of a parliamentary democracy had been laid to the extent that an Act passed a few years later, in 1918, gave the right to vote to 74 per cent of the population. Parliamentary politics was no longer the private preserve of the landed classes as it had been in 1815. Rather, it was now dominated by the representatives of the industrial middle class and the working class.

All of this had happened in the space of a little more than one person's lifetime. However, great though the changes were, we can exaggerate the rapidity of it all if we think of industrialisation as one 'big band' that devastated existing social and economic arrangements. Falling into this trap, the historian Charles Beard, writing in 1901, described the Industrial Revolution as 'a thunderbolt from a clear sky'. In fact Britain had been a trading and commercial nation since at least the sixteenth century. The money that was to be pumped into industry after 1750 had been built up in a process of capital accumulation that stretched back to the development of the cloth trade in the fifteenth century. In the second half of the eighteenth century a series of circumstances coalesced to encourage the investment of that capital in productive industry. Chief among these was a population increase which provided the workforce needed for an industrial economy and, to some extent at least, a market for its goods. Rather than seeing industrialisation as a 'thunderbolt', a better analogy (and one used by W.W. Rostow, a modern economic historian) is that of a jet plane. The British economy may be seen as an aircraft which taxied down the runway for two centuries gradually picking up speed. By 1760 perhaps 30 per cent of the population made their living in trade and manufacture. The final thrust for the aircraft was provided towards the end of the eighteenth century, in the development of the cotton textile industry and the economy took off on its flight into full economic growth.

It may be useful, in thinking of the context from which working-class movements emerged, to divide these years of change into three periods and briefly to identify the determining features of each of them.

a) The Industrial Revolution 1750–1850

There is some dispute over when this phase really began, preceded as it was by such a long period of commercial development, but there is general agreement among historians that the 'Industrial Revolution' was over by 1850. Of course, this does not mean that industrial development had ended by then. After all, an industrial economy is one that is in a perpetual state of growth. But it was clear by the middle of the nineteenth century that the decisive changeover to an industrial economy had been made. By this stage only 22 per cent of the population was engaged in agriculture and there had been an enormous expansion of what were referred to then as the 'industrial districts'. The term reflects the fact that until roughly the 1840s industry tended to be spread over wide areas, often in what are best described as industrial hamlets. The nailmaking villages of the Black Country (part of the West Midlands), provide a good example of this. Today this area consists of a vast urban sprawl, stretching from Birmingham to Wolverhampton but, in the early nineteenth century places like Tipton, Willenhall, Bilston, and Darlaston were distinct villages separated by open countryside. Their inhabitants laboured in their own homes, working up metal supplied by a merchant who would also purchase their completed nails from them. This was the 'putting out' or domestic system, and it was the typical form of production in the early nineteenth century. At the heart of the system were the artisans. These were skilled workers who had often served an apprenticeship and whose skill was a vital resource for an industrialising nation.

In the main this was not a factory workforce. As late as 1850 most people who worked in manufacturing did not work in a factory, nor did their work involve the use of steam-driven machinery. By this date only 300,000 steam-generated horse-power was being used in British industry and over half of this was in the cotton textile factories of Lancashire and Lanarkshire. A comparison with the nine million steam-generated horse-power used by 1907 will confirm that mechanisation was still in its early stages by the end of the Industrial Revolution. Yet the factory was an important feature of this stage of industrialisation because it led to a proliferation of the small workshops that represent the 'typical' working unit. In cotton textiles and in the woollen industry of the West Riding of Yorkshire, factories were developed initially only for the spinning stage of cloth production. Until the advent of machine weaving in the 1830s factory spun yarn was 'put out' to be woven into cloth in the tight-knit hand weaving communities that surrounded towns like Manchester, Glasgow and Leeds. Similarly, the thousands of workshops in Birmingham, making a multitude of small hardware products, and the nailshops of the Black Country, were dependent on the brass and iron supplied from the huge foundries either locally or in South Wales. In Sheffield 30 or 40 steam-driven rolling mills produced the steel that was then farmed out to workshops where it was made up into cutlery.

In this way the factory was the multiplier within industrial production, encouraging the development of the workshop trades rather than, as is sometimes thought, signalling their demise. The geography of industrial production mirrored the distribution of coalfields; the factories were the economic multiplier, and coal fuelled the engines that drove the factories. In 1800 the United Kingdom produced 11 million tons of coal a year. By 1850 this had risen to nearly 50 million tons. This was mostly mined in rural locations in areas such as South Wales and Durham.

Throughout the country the traditional trades were also well represented and these expanded alongside the more obviously industrial trades. For example, despite the centrality of coal to the economy, there were by 1850 more shoemakers in Britain that there were coalminers. For that matter there were more tailors than ironworkers, although this was also the 'Age of Iron'. The various trades that made up the building industry comprised the second largest group of industrial workers after the cotton workers. Needless to say, their methods of work were little different from those used by the building workers in previous centuries. So, by 1850 the British economy was a mixture of new factory-based industries and the outwork industries, located in workshops in the towns or in workers' homes in the industrial villages scattered throughout the countryside.

The development of relatively small, often tightly-knit, communities within the towns and cities bred a fiercely independent workforce. The way industrialisation had taken place through the 'putting out' system meant that working people were used to organising their own worktime. How and when they made up the raw materials supplied by the merchant 'putter out' was up to them. Even in the early factories the workers were generally employed as sub-contracted labour working as a team under the direction of a skilled worker. These teams often paid rent to the factory owner for bench space, steam power, and the cost of heating and lighting the factory. Thus the factory owner was often not the direct employer of labour. This reinforced the sense of independence in the workforce, who geared the amount of work they did to their family needs. They also determined, in large measure *when* they worked. In most trades, for example, it was customary to take Monday as a holiday, the worship of 'Saint Monday' as it was called, and the working year was punctuated by a large number of informal holidays when work would cease. As this would suggest, the culture of these communities was highly integrated. One of the consequences of this was a fairly literate workforce, with the skills of reading and writing often passed on within, and between, families. As the textile manufacturer Richard Cobden explained to a Select Committee in 1838, 'the operatives living so much together, and generally having families, there is usually one in the family or connection who can write'. Education was clearly valued by these communities, though no national system of schooling existed before 1870. Nevertheless, by 1850 two thirds of all children in the five to fourteen age group attended Sunday School, where the rudiments of reading and writing (and even sometimes arithmetic) were taught. A commitment to new nonconformist sects such as Methodism often helped bind these communities together. After 1815 the communities were also being addressed increasingly by the radical newspaper press. Chartism, which demanded political independence for working people, would thrive in the fertile soil provided by these community solidarities and the sense that working people had a right to control their own lives.

The main problem for the industrial middle class lay in converting this, often reluctant, human raw material into a really productive workforce. In justifying the changes that they wished to introduce employers often argued that there was actually no real conflict between the interests of employers and of employees. Once the changes had been introduced they would improve productivity and profits would rise enabling employers to pay better wages. Everybody would benefit, it was argued, from a high profit, high wage economy. In fact, the high incidence of trade union disputes of the period suggest either that there really was a fundamental conflict of interests between the two groups, or that the compatibility of their interests was not always readily apparent. In order to stress the closeness of the two classes industrialists often portrayed themselves as workmen who had made good by their own efforts. As the steam engine manufacturer Matthew Boulton put it, 'All the manufacturers I have ever known began the world with small capitals'. In fact, Boulton inherited his factory from his father and was of a sufficiently high social status to marry a woman with a dowry of £28,000! Stressing hard work as a factor in the creation of industrial fortunes was seen as a way of establishing role models for the working class. Sir Titus Salt was a wealthy woollen cloth manufacturer, who became mayor and then MP for the town of Bradford. His nineteenth-century biographer put his success down to early rising and punctuality!

Obviously, there was a little more to the growing wealth of the middle class than these smug assessments of the successful would suggest. These were generally men who inherited small amounts of capital that had been carefully nurtured in their families for generations. They were sometimes nonconformists, shut out of public life because of legal restrictions on people of their religion, who concentrated their energies on commerce. Their abstemious lifestyles (compared with the eighteenth-century landed classes) accelerated the process of capital accumulation. When economic circumstances became favourable in the late eighteenth century they were well placed to invest their capital in productive industry. Some, such as the elder Robert Peel (father of the future prime minister, whose textile firm made him a millionaire), became spectacularly wealthy. But most of the really wealthy men in Britain were landowners and this applied throughout the nineteenth century. A recent survey concludes that the successful manufacturer at death left an estate of around £100,000. Two fairly typical examples are John Bright, the textile manufacturer, MP, and Anti-Corn Law League organiser, who died in 1889 leaving £86,000 and Joseph Chamberlain, screw manufacturer, mayor of Birmingham and MP for the borough, who died in 1914 leaving £125,000. Invariably, these estates would have included land and property.

This was a group who saw themselves as 'self-made', without the privileged position and upbringing of the landed classes. Wealth, they argued, was the reward for endeavour by the individual. Their ideal was a society within which they would be unfettered in their enterprises by either the government or trade unions. In this way the market would determine the level of prices and wages. These were the men who came to dominate the growing towns, which they saw as their territory in the way that the aristocracy expected to control the countryside.

Most of the reform movements that developed during the period of the Industrial Revolution reflected an antipathy between the two classes. Before 1850 this was exacerbated by a tendency for the immature industrial economy to veer swiftly between boom and slump conditions. Economic crisis invariably exposed the separate interests of the two classes. Despite this, there was always the possibility that the middle and working classes could be led to act together in movements for radical change, particularly if a privileged aristocracy could be portrayed as the villain of the piece. The aristocracy dominated the political system both nationally through the Houses of Parliament, and locally as magistrates, lords lieutenant of the counties and Guardians of the Poor. In parliament these wealthy landowners divided themselves into Whigs and Tories and this provided the party framework for the formation of governments and the settling of political issues. These were simply rival factions. They were loose groupings of family connections, rather than political parties in the modern sense of highly structured organisations with contrasting ideologies. During the late eighteenth and early nineteenth centuries enough differences between the two groups had emerged for administrations to take on a party complexion; the Whigs were traditionally supporters of limited parliamentary reform and religious tolerance whilst the Tories were characterised by their defence of church and king. But both were aristocratic in their composition and outlook; well over half the MPs in both parties were from landed backgrounds. Nevertheless, the reforming tradition within the Whigs made them more aware than the Tories in 1830 that the cost of continuing to exclude the middle class from the vote was the possibility that they might then ally with the, similarly excluded, working class. In the Reform Bill campaign and all subsequent movements working-class leaders had to decide if their interests would be best served by co-operation with the middle class or by opposing them outright.

b) The Workshop of the World 1850–85

From about the mid-1840s the British economy expanded. Some economic historians have questioned the existence of a 'mid-Victorian boom', but this is what it must have felt like at the time. The scale of many industries increased as did the degree of mechanisation. The output of coal trebled in the period. The canal system was replaced by a nationwide railway network at vast expense, all borne by private capital. Britain drew a huge advantage from having been the world's first industrial nation. During this period vast amounts of capital, skill and industrial goods were despatched to all corners of the globe, as Britain became the 'workshop of the world'. The 1851 census revealed that 54 per cent of the population now lived in towns and this percentage steadily increased thereafter.

With expanding trade came increasing mechanisation and a greater need, on the part of employers, to control and maintain production levels. This meant exerting greater discipline over the workforce. As one Birmingham manufacturer put it in 1867:

> When we started a steam engine, I told the people it would be necessary to begin at a fixed hour, instead of the irregularity which had been usual. The men objected very much ...

This extension of labour discipline could have involved great conflict. Yet much had been learned about labour relations during the preceding period. Now employers attempted to gain compliance by arriving at mutual agreements with the most skilled (and therefore most important) of their labour force. As a result this was a period when the skilled elite of the working class, sometimes called the 'aristocracy of labour', were able to extract concessions in the form of higher wages and better conditions. They also won the vote by a Reform Act in 1867, and legal status for their trade unions by legislation in the 1870s. A flourishing economy could afford a spirit of conciliation between employers and at least their most skilled employees. This new relationship was reflected in support for the Liberal Party from what was seen as the 'respectable' working class.

c) International Competition 1885–1914

In these years a number of nations challenged Britain's industrial dominance. This competition was acted out in an unseemly scramble for overseas territory between the European powers, which presaged a wider conflict to come at the end of the period in the shape of the First World War. At home industrial growth slowed and, since this occurred alongside continued population growth, this made unemployment an endemic problem. Employers furiously tried to make their firms more competitive on the international stage, by re-organising production to increase output, and this inevitably led to the rebirth of militant trade unionism. The 'new unionism' of the 1890s and the 'labour unrest' of 1910–14 involved a more extensive workforce than had previously existed. In these circumstances, a concerted movement from a hostile labour force carried severe implications for social stability.

d) Working-Class Movements and Social and Economic Change

The broad context for the achievement of citizenship by working people was created by the long process of economic development which changed an agricultural society into an industrial-urban society. Yet, this is not to argue that economic change *caused* the particular reforms that took place in this period. To argue thus would be to adopt a 'reductionist' position whereby human activity is seen as pre-determined by economic processes. All historical situations are more complex than this; economic reductionism robs our historical characters of their freedom of choice in particular circumstances. Yet most historians would agree that in this period economic and social developments were linked in some way. It is for this reason that the economic and social history of nineteenth- and twentieth-century Britain are so frequently to be found together on the same course syllabus. It is perhaps useful to think of economic change as creating the framework of opportunity within which social relations were then acted out, rather than as a decisive force pre-determining outcomes. The successes and failures of the reform movements identified in this book came about because individuals and groups made particular decisions in specific circumstances. By the same token, however, we can rarely explain history only in terms of the immediate context. Take as an example of this the many explanations for the failure of Chartism that will be discussed in Chapter 3. It is often tempting to settle the matter swiftly by saying that there was really only one reason

why Chartism failed: because Parliament rejected the Chartist petition. Of course, such an explanation would only reformulate the
question 'why did Chartism fail?' into 'why did Parliament reject the
Charter?' To answer such a question properly historians need to
understand not only the long-term causes (like the impact of economic change), and the short-term causes (perhaps the intervention of
an individual, an organisation or an idea), but also the way these
interrelated at a particular moment in time. The most obvious way in
which this coalescence manifested itself was in the expression of
social attitudes between the various groups that made up society. The
developments that will be examined in this book were a reflection of
the framework of values and belief through which these social groups
perceived each other. This raises the knotty issue of 'class'.

3 'Class' and the Historians

> **KEY ISSUE** How can historians use the term 'class' in such a way
> as to capture the contemporary meaning of the term?

The use of the term 'class' is the subject of much debate by historians
and it is worth trying to clarify some of the issues, since the term is
employed throughout this book. A helpful starting point may be to
note that all historians use 'class' in some way or other. That is to say,
nobody argues that this was a society made up of an undifferentiated
mass of people or that it was simply an agglomeration of individuals.
In the period under study there was a very clear awareness of the
social differences between the groups that made up society. Victorian
literature abounds with heroes or heroines agonising over the issue,
perhaps in relation to a marriage outside their class that might be considered 'beneath them'. Nor was it considered a great problem that
society should incorporate vast differences of wealth and prospects in
its component parts. On the contrary, social inequality was rather celebrated in a society which had convinced itself that the opportunities
were available for anybody to move from 'rags to riches' through hard
work and moral rectitude. From this point of view wealth and status
provided important indicators of an individual's morality. Social class
was important for people at the time and therefore constitutes an
important medium for the historian's understanding of the period.

   Despite this area of consensus, historians still disagree over the
implications of class divisions for the process of historical change. For
example, given that classes existed, were they necessarily forever in
conflict? The nineteenth-century political thinker Karl Marx argued
that they were. He identified class conflict as growing logically out of
the nature of capitalist society. Employers made their profits by
exploiting labour and therefore the interests of the two classes were

doomed always to be at odds. At its simplest, when wages went up profits went down, and this polarity of interests produced a necessarily hostile relationship between the two groups. Following this, Marxist historians, such as Edward Thompson and Eric Hobsbawm, have explored those areas of conflict between the classes as the most significant for historical analysis.

Alternatively, some historians share the view of many contemporary observers, that relationships between workers and employers were always at least potentially harmonious, since an industrial society could operate to the benefit of both groups. High profits meant increased investment, more jobs and higher wages, so conflict was not inevitable. Where it occurred it was not a product of the system, but rather the impact of other influences, perhaps economic crisis, or war, or simply misunderstandings that could be rectified by better education. These liberal historians tend to stress the points of mutual agreement between the classes as the really important moments in any historical period. Presenting this approach in his book *The Origins of Modern English Society 1780–1880,* Harold Perkin argues that by the mid-Victorian period the relations between the classes were 'those of a familiar kind of marriage in which the partners cannot live without bickering but are perfectly aware that apart they cannot live at all'.

The significance of this difference of interpretation for an understanding of the period 1815–1914 relates primarily to the issue of exactly how much political solidarity and enthusiasm the working class displayed at any given moment. Liberal historians stress the fragmentation of the working class, sometimes preferring the term 'working classes'. They point out that this social group consisted of a variety of trades spread over a wide area and such disparity worked against a common view being either held or expressed. Trade unions, with their concern for the members of one trade, are generally cited as an example of this sectionalism. Where wider protest movements emerged, such as Chartism, they are seen by liberal historians as being more regional than national expressions. The failure of such movements is seen as proof that their exponents lacked any class consciousness.

Historians on the political left argue that despite the differences of regions and trades within the working class it was still united by a common experience of industrialisation. Working people were tied together by exploitation at work, material deprivation, political exclusion and the hostility of the law to their organisations. Movements such as Chartism are seen as evidence of this universal perception of society, held throughout by the working class. Trade unions, though concerned with the interests of particular trades, still brought a common class consciousness to bear on their members' problems. Wider organisations such as Chartism and the Labour Party, it is argued, were the expressions of a growing sense that those who shared this common experience and consciousness should band together to improve their position.

Returning to our original image of labour's achievement of citizenship as a journey, how do these two, very different interpretations map out the itinerary? Left-wing historians see this as a perilous journey, with each mile travelled at huge cost. Hard won gains could easily be lost since the terrain remained hostile. Thus, trade unions had to win the fight for their legality not once but three times, in 1824, 1875 and 1906. Male suffrage, rejected in 1839, 1842 and 1848, was ostensibly gained in 1884. But the vote was deliberately given in such a way that, in practice, large numbers of working men remained outside the electorate until 1918.

From a liberal perspective, however, each gain represented a step towards a more rational society based on consent and understanding (and a private enterprise economy). The Chartists, it is argued, simply wanted too much too soon. Change came gradually and was conceded as people demonstrated their readiness for citizenship. This produced a gradual and fairly smooth transition to a modern society in a series of well defined steps marked by the Reform Acts of 1832, 1867, 1884, 1918, and 1928. This, of course, raises all sorts of questions, such as, 'In what sense were the working class "not ready" for the vote in 1839?' or, 'Why were women "not ready" for the vote on a basis of equality with men until 1928?'

As the story is unfolded in the chapters that follow, these differences of interpretation will be picked out, where appropriate, and commented upon. But what is clear is that any social class consists of a large number of often very different groups. The new middle class ranged from shopkeepers to merchant bankers, and from clerks to industrialists. Similarly, 'working class' is a label that may be applied to individuals as disparate as the highly skilled, and well paid engineering worker, right down to the wretched inmate of the Union Workhouse. It is assumed in this book that it is possible to identify values, aspirations and beliefs that tie these social groups together and enable historians to refer meaningfully, as contemporaries did, to both 'the working class' and 'the middle class'. This is not to say, however, that all members of these classes always acted in similar ways or that they always saw their identities as being exactly the same as those of other members of the social group to which they belonged.

For the early historians of working-class movements, like G.D.H. Cole or John and Barbara Hammond, who were themselves active in the Labour Party, it seemed clear that the 'journey' was always taking the working class towards the Labour Party's version of socialism. In fact, we know that there were also working-class Liberals and Conservatives in the nineteenth century. For left-wing social historians, like E.P. Thompson and Eric Hobsbawm, writing in the 1960s and the 1970s, the hope was that socialism would transform society. Yet, in the 1970s and the 1980s sections of the British working class voted in support of Margaret Thatcher and the Conservative Party. Historians writing in the wake of Thatcherism have tended to stress the diversity of working-class identities in any given period. If working-class history is seen simply as a journey towards socialism, it would seem that a wrong turn was taken somewhere along the road. As Rohan McWilliam explains in his book *Popular Politics in Nineteenth Century England* (1998, p 26), the social historians of the 1960s and 1970s tended to see 'class' identity, once formed as fixed and immutable:

> The traditional narrative had assumed that there were such things as autonomous class cultures and a working class ideology ... Too often, this ideology was assumed to be socialism, and popular politics became simply the story of how the working class came to discover socialism.

Within any organisation formed to express the views of either the middle or the working classes there was always a tension between the commonly shared perspective and the different interests of the various groups that made up the class. At times, for example, a carpenters' trade union may appear to argue the case for the working class, calling for votes for working men or a 'living wage' for all. At other times it may argue the trade's case, calling for better wages for carpenters (apparently at the expense of other trades). Trade unions frequently acted for male workers against the interests of women workers in the same trade. Probably, the major revision of the term 'class' by historians of the nineteenth century is to move away from the idea that class-consciousness is a single dimensional identity. Most of the working-class movements examined here exhibit this oscillation between class solidarity and fragmentation. As subsequent chapters will demonstrate, there were periods when circumstances determined that the expression of a 'class identity' meant membership of a mass-based movement like Chartism. At other times, the identity of 'the trade' became more important, as is evident in the mid-Victorian period.

Rather than chasing a fixed version of 'class consciousness' in our historical analysis, it is more helpful to focus on the achievement of status of full citizenship for working people over the last 200 years. This is the primary objective of this book. We should not underestimate that achievement nor the contribution made towards it in the period under study here. A Labour government entered office in 1924, only a decade after the close of our period. In a little over a century working people had moved from an almost total exclusion from the political system to a position where they were running the country.

Working on Chapter 1

This chapter has introduced you to two ideas: first, that reform movements were related in some way to the economic and social context in which they grew and thus should be seen through the eyes of the participants, and second, that labour's 'journey' to citizenship can be interpreted from a number of points of view. Notes arranged under the following headings will help you to capture these points:

1. The changing context. What were the major features of social and economic change in the period
   a) the Industrial Revolution 1750–1850
   b) the Workshop of the World 1850–85
   c) international competition 1885–1914?

2. Class and the historians. Why do historians disagree over class?

3. Labour's road to citizenship.
   a) what are the difficulties with this metaphor (paras 1–4 in the chapter)?
   b) define the 'journey' seen by left-wing historians.
   c) define the 'journey' seen by liberal historians.
   d) How has the approach to 'class' been recently refined?

2 The Reform Act and Before: Reform Movements 1815–32

POINTS TO CONSIDER

This chapter explores the popular agitation for Parliamentary reform from the closing of the Napoleonic Wars to the passing of the Reform Act. Looking back from the present day we often see the Reform Act of 1832 as the first step on the road to democracy, to be complemented by further Acts in 1867 and 1884. This was not the way it would have looked at the time. Between 1815 and 1820 radicals like Heny Hunt and William Cobbett evolved a comprehensive set of political demands, based on a late eighteenth century critique of the political system. The Reform Act delivered much less than this programme aspired to achieve; in fact, the Act's originators in Parliament saw it as a way to prevent democracy (and the achievement of the wider programme of popular radicalism) rather than promoting it. To understand the 'class' politics of Chartism you will need to see the Reform Act through the eyes of the post-war radicals, as a compromise which delivered little.

KEY DATES

1815 End of the Napoleonic Wars; start of a five-year economic recession.

1816 Establishment of Hampden Clubs; Henry Hunt holds reform meetings in Spa Fields, London.

1817 Gagging Acts passed; March of the Blanketeers (Lancashire); Pentridge Uprising (Derbyshire).

1819 'Peterloo' massacre (Manchester); the Six Acts passed to supress the radical movement.

1820 Cato Street Conspiracy (London).

1827 Death of Lord Liverpool.

1828 Wellington becomes Prime Minister; moves are made to disenfranchise the 'rotten boroughs' of Penryn and East Retford.

1829 Roman Catholic Emancipation is passed, following pressure from the Catholic Association.

1830 Formation of the Birmingham Political Union under Thomas Attwood; Wellington's government falls over reform; Whigs take office and propose a Reform Bill; 'Swing Riots' over rural economic grievances, in the south.

1831 Countrywide reform meetings and Political Unions formed throughout the country, including the National Political Union in London under Francis Place.

1832 'Days of May' crisis; Reform Bill enacted and a General Election held; Attwood elected to Parliament.

1833 Legislation by the reformed Parliament, including the Irish
–5 Coercion Act (1833) and the New Poor Law (1834) confirm the radicals' disappointment with the effects of the Reform Act.

'Damn Earl Grey's bloody head off'. These six words scrawled on a wall in the centre of Birmingham in May 1833, and noted by a visitor to the town, testified eloquently to the sense of frustration created in the working population by the 1832 Reform Act. As Prime Minister, and leader of the Whigs, Grey had steered the Reform Act through its difficult parliamentary passage, to enormous popular acclaim in Birmingham and the nation as a whole only a year before. Now he was the subject of popular criticism throughout the country as it became clear that the reform of Parliament, brought about by the Act, did not match the high expectations of its working-class supporters. The pattern of these expectations had been acquired by working people in the period between 1815 and 1820, when the demand for the vote had gained widespread support in the industrial districts. Access to national politics had been increasingly believed to be a way by which labour could control its own destiny in a period of economic change. But the movement of 1815–20 had failed to achieve its primary objective of votes for all men over the age of 21 (universal manhood suffrage). The much more limited Reform Bill, proposed by the Whigs in 1831, had been supported by working people because it had seemed to offer at least a first step towards a more radically democratised system. But a year after its passage it had become clear that the Act was intended as a 'once and for all' adjustment to stabilise the system and preserve the inequalities of the pre-reform structure of representation.

Most working people were excluded from the political system by the requirement, both before and after 1832, that voters should own a substantial amount of property of one sort or another. Thus, whilst the Industrial Revolution changed workers' lives dramatically, they had little access to the political structures that controlled those changes. The Marxist historian E.P. Thompson has argued in his book *The Making of the English Working Class* (1963) that a growing awareness of this political exclusion was a crucial element in converting the eighteenth-century 'labouring poor' into the nineteenth-century 'working class'. In his view the 1832 Reform Act represents a crucial historical moment in this change. By this Act the new middle class were given the vote whilst, broadly speaking, working people remained voteless. The workforce created by industrialisation was now unified, he argues, not only by its economic role but also by its political isolation. Many historians would contest this hypothesis arguing that Thompson overstates the cohesion of the working community and that 1832 is too early to speak of a working-class consciousness with its own distinctive point of view on the political and economic system. However, what does seem certain is that from the end of the Napoleonic Wars to the demise of Chartism, in about 1850, there was support for a radical reform of the Parliamentary system from working people on an unprecedented scale. Economic change had made politics an issue in ways it had never been previously.

1 The Unreformed Parliamentary System

> **KEY ISSUES** In what ways was the pre-Reform political system considered to be 'representative' and on what basis did radicals evolve a critique of the system based on late eighteenth-century alternative concepts of 'representation?

a) 'Old Corruption': The Unreformed House of Commons in 1830

British government revolved round the monarchy, the House of Lords and the House of Commons. The House of Commons controlled finances, although the monarch and the Lords possessed the right to reject (veto) legislation introduced by the lower house. As the centre-piece of the system, the Commons drew its authority from its elected status. British government, therefore, was focused upon a legislative body, the Commons, which saw itself as representative of the nation. Yet just how representative of the people of the United Kingdom was the House of Commons before 1832?

After the Act of Union was passed in 1800, the Irish Parliament was abolished and Irish representation was transferred to Westminster. There were now 658 Members of Parliament sitting in the Commons. As the table below demonstrates, by 1830 the distribution of these MPs was distorted in England's favour in terms of the ratio of MPs to population size.

The English MPs made up well over two-thirds of the House of Commons. Four of these members represented the Universities of Oxford and Cambridge. The rest of the English members came from two types of constituency, the counties and the Parliamentary boroughs. The size of the electorate in each of these constituencies

	No. of MPs	MP–Population ratio
England	485	1 MP per 27,000 people
Wales	24	1 MP per 33,000 people
Scotland	45	1 MP per 53,000 people
Ireland	100	1 MP per 77,000 people

varied greatly as did the nature of the voting qualification (franchise). In the 40 English counties, electing a total of 82 MPs, the vote was held by individuals owning freehold land valued at 40 shillings per year for the purposes of the Poor rates.

The Parliamentary boroughs were mostly towns which had been granted the right to elect MPs at some time, often in the distant past. These were numerically the most significant of all constituencies since they accounted for 403 of the total MPs in the Commons. In the boroughs the franchise varied widely and was often of antique origin. For example, in the 38 'scot and lot' boroughs the franchise was held by any man who paid poor rates. Here the electorate was often numerous and indeed the borough of Westminster had 10,000 voters. Yet 24 of these boroughs had fewer than 600 voters, the most extreme case being Gatton in Surrey. This consisted of only six houses, the owner of which was free to nominate two MPs. In the 'burgage' boroughs the vote was held by virtue of ownership of particular pieces of land and none of the 35 constituencies in this category possessed more than 300 electors. In fact, Old Sarum in Wiltshire possessed no voters at all. In this case, whoever owned the piece of land, which the radical journalist William Cobbett referred to as the 'Accursed Hill', also nominated two MPs. In Dunwich, a 'freeman' borough in Suffolk, few of the 30 men, qualified to vote by virtue of their status as freemen of the borough, actually lived in the constituency. One could hardly blame them, most of Dunwich having long since disappeared under the North Sea as a result of coastal erosion, and being visible only at low tide!

The problem of Parliamentary representation might be summarised as follows. Most MPs in the House of Commons were elected by the English boroughs. Over half of these had under 600 electors and the majority were located in the south of the country. Although in the early nineteenth century most of the population still lived in this area, with industrialisation it became increasingly clear that the existing representation reflected the economic structure of an earlier age. The large towns of the Midlands and North, which grew from the mid eighteenth century as a result of industrialisation, were often unrepresented, except by their county members. Put alongside the unenfranchised status of, say, Manchester, Leeds and Birmingham, the smallness of most borough electorates was increasingly difficult to justify.

There was widespread concern at the corruptness of the electoral procedure and this was most marked in the constituencies with small electorates. A majority of seats were uncontested, with the patron's nominee being returned to Parliament unchallenged. There was no secret ballot and voters were likely to be bribed or intimidated into voting for particular candidates. Even in the counties, where electorates tended to be larger, the voters were mostly tenant farmers who also owned the small piece of land which gave them the right to vote. They invariably found it 'convenient' to vote for the candidate nominated by their landlord. Failure to do so might result in eviction or a rent increase. In the boroughs votes and seats were openly bought and sold, and where a small electorate made this a simple procedure (as in, among others, Gatton, Dunwich or Old Sarum) the constituencies were termed 'nomination boroughs', 'pocket boroughs' or, more graphically, 'rotten boroughs'. Ownership of a borough could bring social status and perhaps the material rewards of government positions, sinecures or pensions for the owner and his dependants, in return for Parliamentary support for a particular Party or measure. The market in seats was extensive; one authority calculated in 1827 that 276 seats were held by direct nomination and many more were subject to influence. Involvement in politics could be a very expensive activity; Gatton, for example, changed hands for the last time in 1830, for £180,000. In the counties it was complained that the large size of the electorate, and the need to 'treat' the electors, made standing for Parliament a costly business. Not surprisingly, most MPs were either themselves from the English landed classes, or were their appointed agents and were dependent upon their patronage.

In his book Voters, Patrons and Parties (1989), Frank O'Gorman suggests that our view of the eighteenth-century political system may be distorted by our own commitment to a very different form of representation in the present-day political system. In tracing the emergence of a mass electorate in the nineteenth and twentieth centuries, historians have demonised, to the point of distortion, the unreformed system by which it was preceded. He challenges the view that votes were simply bought and sold and that there was no wider participation in the electoral process. Eighteenth-century elections were very open affairs in the sense that whole communities turned out to watch the voting and to try to influence the proceedings. Whilst voters were open to persuasion (including financial inducements), they saw themselves as exercising a high degree of independent choice. He argues that, 'Elections put on a public display and in a very real sense held to public account the governing elite, their clients, dependants and supporters'. From this point of view, the eighteenth-century electoral system may have contributed significantly to social stability. O'Gorman's work reminds us that we should try to understand the pre-reform system in the terms it was seen at the time. Nevertheless, much of the context in which the old system operated was changing by the start of the nineteenth century. The structure of the wealthy elite was changing in the localities, the exclusion of industrial wealth was widely condemned and working people increasingly wanted a formal role in the political process.

b) Critics and Supporters, of the Unreformed System

Looking back from the vantage point of a modern liberal democracy, the shortcomings of the early nineteenth-century House of Commons as a representative institution seem clear enough. Only about five per cent of the total population of the United Kingdom voted. Women were excluded. The men who voted did so through a confusing variety of, often archaic, franchises with most of the representatives coming from the south of England. It appears to us a system ripe for reform, but how did it appear to contemporaries?

Of course, contemporaries did not look at the system from the position of a twentieth-century liberal democracy. In the main, influential opinion (that is, the view of those with wealth) seems to have seen this simply as a problem of distortion within a basically sound structure. Indeed the unreformed system was widely defended on the grounds that it was representative. In 1790 the respected Whig statesman Edmund Burke put it this way:

> 1 We know that the British House of Commons, without shutting its doors to any merit in any class, is by the sure operation of adequate causes, filled with everything illustrious in rank, in descent, in hereditary and in acquired opulence, in cultivated talents, in military, civil, naval and
> 5 politic distinction that the country can afford.

In 1810 Lord Liverpool, soon to be Tory Prime Minister, was similarly struck by the openness of the British political system: 'There never was a period in our history when the representation of the people in Parliament was less unequal'. As late as 1830 the Duke of Wellington, as Prime Minister, was happy to assure the House of Lords that 'he was fully convinced that the country possessed at the present moment, a legislature which answered all the good purposes of legislation'.

The Duke, of course, was a quite spectacular reactionary and few, by 1830, shared his view of the perfection of the existing Parliamentary structure. On the other hand, few among the propertied classes wished to tear down the structure and begin again on different principles. The strength of the unreformed system, from this viewpoint, was that it did represent and support wealth, very directly and reasonably efficiently. MPs were required to fulfil a property qualification and while the franchises may have been confusingly disparate most were based on property ownership in some form. Nor was the system necessarily exclusive since anybody, irrespective of rank and status, could purchase a rotten borough provided they had the money. Given the recent example of the French Revolution, this was as close to egalitarianism as many wished to venture.

For Burke, Liverpool and Wellington the absurdities of Old Sarum, Gatton and so forth were simply the endearing eccentricities of an evolving political system that had stood the test of time and which worked. Government, they argued, should represent, not numbers of population as we should expect, but rather the significant *interests* in the nation, such as Land, the City of London, the Universities, the corporate towns, and the Church. If these interest groups were represented at Westminster then, the argument ran, a nation was represented. For most people, of course, this system would give only a *virtual representation* of their interests rather than a direct representation. Most importantly, the rich would represent the poor. Very few among the wealthy disputed this definition of representative government. However, after 1815, it was being argued increasingly that industrialisation had created a new interest group in the industrial middle class. It was the exclusion of this new interest that was most widely recognised as the problem. The 1832 Reform Act was designed to rectify this problem and not to remodel the system itself or the principles upon which it was based.

It is important to note that this impetus for reform existed within the wealthy classes and was particularly evident in the new industrial middle class. However, there was another, quite separate, critique of the political system being offered in this period which made very different assumptions about the nature of representative government. This was, perhaps, most effectively argued in Britain by Thomas Paine in his book the *Rights of Man* (1791), which was written to counter Burke's earlier defence of the system. Drawing on *his* experience of both the American and French Revolutions, Paine argued that the corruption of the British Parliamentary system lay in its failure to represent 'the people' in any direct sense. He claimed that while most of the country was crippled by taxation, the small minority who controlled politics lived off the proceeds of taxation. This state of affairs was perpetuated by the restriction of the right to vote to a small section of the population. The vote, he argued, was a 'natural right' to which every man was entitled and which had been taken away at some point in the distant past. If this right was restored it would lead to the regaining of other important freedoms. Among these he numbered the freedoms of expression, assembly, conscience and equality before the law. Paine argued his case in terms of men only. It fell to another writer in the same tradition, Mary Wollstonecraft, to point out, in her book *A Vindication of the Rights of Woman* (1792), that if there really were 'natural rights', then women were also entitled to exercise them.

Paine's book was said to have sold 200,000 copies by 1793. The government, recognising its subversive nature, declared it illegal and by so doing increased its popularity enormously. At the heart of Paine's alternative vision of the political world lay the belief that participation in politics should not be determined by the ownership of property and that the government really should represent 'the people'. For Burke, on the other hand, the art of government was a body of wisdom to be carefully passed from one generation to the next. Suddenly to extend the franchise would admit individuals to government who knew nothing of its complexities. In this case he said, in a classic statement:

> Along with its natural protectors and guardians, learning will be cast into the mire, and trodden under the hoofs of a swinish multitude.

This celebrated reference by Burke to 'a swinish multitude' reminds us that in excluding the propertyless, the existing system was based upon a very unflattering view of the working community. When we examine the statements of working-class reformers, in this and later periods, it is clear that their objection to the political system was not simply that it excluded them, but also that their unfranchised status was justified in such deprecatory, inaccurate, and offensive terms.

Paine argued that ordinary people were both entitled to, and capable of, political participation. By 1820 this approach had been eagerly taken up by radicals who used it as the basis for a reform programme which called for universal manhood suffrage, annual Parliaments and vote by secret ballot. The strength of these demands will be examined in this chapter and the next. Yet the distinction should be made at the outset between Parliamentary reform in order to achieve simply a place in the system for the industrial interest alone *and* those who approached political reform from the kind of perspectives defined by Paine. As we shall see, the most threatening aspect of the *1832* Reform Bill campaign lay in the way it drew together the advocates of these two distinct ways of looking at politics behind a single, unified, demand.

2 Agitation and Repression 1815–20

> **KEY ISSUES** Why did radicalism grow in the period following the end of the Napoleonic Wars and how was this dealt with by the government?

a) The Growth of Popular Politics

Between 1793 and 1815 Britain was, with one brief respite, continually at war with France. This acted as a catalyst upon the British economy, which found itself with an increased demand for the products of its main industries of textiles, metalware, mining, shipbuilding and, in particular, agriculture. Capital investment was encouraged and employers took to reorganising their enterprises to increase productivity. But peace ushered in a period of recession as demand fell, troops were demobilised and the labouring population found itself unemployed. Parliament, consisting largely of landowners, passed the Corn Law of 1815 prohibiting the importation of foreign corn until home grown corn reached 80 shillings per quarter. This was intended to ensure that the price of corn and therefore bread remained high. Increasing numbers of working people found themselves dependent upon parish relief for the basic necessities of life.

The immediate post-war years also witnessed a growth of Painite political radicalism as the working population increasingly regarded their economic position in political terms. Often the lead was taken by 'gentlemen reformers', members of the upper class who, unlike most of their social equals, accepted the importance of a really extensive parliamentary reform. For example, John Cartwright established the Hampden Club, in London in 1812, to agitate for what was called a 'general suffrage'. Cartwright was an eccentric landed gentleman from Lincolnshire who had been active in radical politics since the American Revolution in the 1770s. It was his belief that manhood suffrage and other political rights had been lost by Englishmen at the time of the Norman conquest in 1066. Though he never attracted the 'respectable' support he hoped for in London itself, the idea was taken up with energy in the provinces. Over the next few years Hampden Clubs were set up by working people in towns and villages in the industrial areas of Lancashire, the Midlands and Yorkshire. They were open to any man able to pay the weekly subscription of a penny, this money being devoted to the publication of pamphlets and broadsides supporting the radical cause.

In November and December 1816 Henry Hunt held three large public meetings in Spa-Fields in London calling for universal manhood suffrage and parliamentary reform. Hunt, the son of a Wiltshire farmer, was undoubtedly the leading radical of the day. It was he, more than anyone else, who popularised the mass meeting as a means of reform agitation. But at the second of 'Orator' Hunt's Spa-Fields meetings a part of the crowd rioted. The following January the ever unpopular Prince Regent was mobbed returning from the opening of Parliament and the window of his coach was smashed. Lord Liverpool's Tory administration, fearful of the implications of Hampden Club activity in the provinces, used these two incidents as a basis for introducing repressive legislation, which came to be known as the 'Gagging Acts'. *Habeas Corpus* was suspended for four months (allowing arrest and imprisonment on suspicion only), and restrictions on public meetings were extended. The Hampden Clubs were effectively outlawed.

Above all else the government feared a re-enactment of the French Revolution on British soil. Their concern focused on the growth of support among the artisans for these political clubs. In fact, radical organisations were more concerned to obtain redress by using the constitutional right to petition Parliament rather than overthrowing the State by force of arms. The parliamentary session of 1817 saw the submission of nearly 700 petitions for reform in a national campaign co-ordinated by Sir Francis Burdett. Burdett, a Leicestershire landowner, was a gentleman-reformer and radical MP for Westminster. His 1817 petitioning campaign demonstrated the scope of the agitation for reform. From industrial districts in the Midlands, the North, Lanarkshire, South Wales and the West Country, fearful magistrates were reporting radical activity amongst the working classes. Although support was still widely dispersed throughout the country, it was beginning to come together. In March 1817 a group of

Lancashire weavers set out to march to London to present their petition personally, intending to hold meetings on the way and to draw in numbers for a tumultuous entry into the capital. This was the 'March of the Blanketeers', so called because each man carried only a blanket and provisions for the journey. However, the marchers were soon turned back and their leaders were arrested.

In their concern over insurrection the government employed an *agent provocateur,* a spy code-named 'Oliver', to travel through the country making contact with radical groups. He pretended to be planning a rebellion and in this way hoped to draw local activists into the open, where they could be arrested. This resulted in the tragedy of the 'Pentridge Uprising' of 9 June 1817 when 200–300 armed working men from the remote Derbyshire weaving village of Pentridge marched on Nottingham, thinking they were part of Oliver's national rebellion. They were easily dispersed and Jeremiah Brandreth, the stocking weaver who was their leader, was later executed.

In August 1819 the Yeomanry, a part-time military force drawn from the local middle class, broke up a large but peaceful meeting in St. Peter's Fields, Manchester. Somewhere between 50,000 and 200,000 people had gathered to hear Henry Hunt speak in favour of universal suffrage. Eleven died at 'Peterloo' and over 400 were injured, many of them women and children. Lord Liverpool's government praised the Yeomanry and passed the Six Acts. These suppressed the popular movement by restricting public meetings, tightening the definition of seditious libel (to restrict what radical papers could publish about the government), increasing the tax on newspapers (to hit the working-class readership of radical journals) and extending the right to enter and search private premises. Successful prosecution of radicals increased dramatically, in both London and the provinces.

The imprisonment of leading radicals broke up the reform organisation, while an improvement in trade eroded mass support in the early 1820s. In the face of the government's firmness, parliamentary reform was unlikely to advance further. On the other hand, improved trade opened up the possibility of using trade union organisations to gain better conditions. In fact, the arrest and execution in 1820 of Arthur Thistlewood and his three collaborators, for their part in the 'Cato Street conspiracy' to kill the members of the Cabinet, marks a convenient closing point for this period of agitation. We may now consider its significance.

b) The Legacy of the Post-War Years

This period of agitation saw the emergence of a political programme which drew on the imagery of the French Revolution and the ideas of Paine. By 1820 reformers were concerned with universal suffrage, annual parliaments, and vote by secret ballots, as well as the disenfranchisement of the rotten boroughs. These concerns would later be the basis of working-class demands in Chartism. The period also demonstrated the importance of the radical press in carrying ideas to disparate geographical areas. The poet Southey warned the Prime Minister in 1817 that William Cobbett's radical weekly paper *The Political Register* was read aloud in every ale-house.

Above all, however, the great lesson of the agitation lay in its vulnerability to government repression. 'Oliver' and 'Peterloo' made subsequent radical movements fear a direct attack by the State. The Chartists, for example, expected such action and argued that force might legitimately be used defensively in such cases. Also, although the post-war movement attracted its share of gentlemen reformers, such as Cartwright and Burdett, its strength lay in the support of artisans and other workers in industrial towns and villages. The new middle class, although also at this time excluded from political life, took little part in this campaign as they feared its implications for law and order and did not share the enthusiasm for votes for the unpropertied. The ease with which Liverpool's government contained the campaign by positive action emphasised the fact that a popular movement could always be vulnerable to repression without the extensive support of the wealthy. George Edmonds, a radical journalist imprisoned for a year for his reforming activities in 1820, explained to a public meeting ten years later, at the start of the Reform Bill campaign: 'He would tell them that the remonstrances of 1,000 men with each £1,000 in their pockets, were far more influential with their present government than the just complaints of 10,000 men not possessed of a farthing but suffering and starving through their iniquitous system of misrule and corruption.'

3 The Reform Bill Campaign 1830–32

> **KEY ISSUES** Why did working people support the campaign for a Reform Act in 1830–32 and how close did the country come to revolution in these years?

a) Political Changes

During the late 1820s sections of the urban middle class were drawn into the movement to reform Parliament. Trade had improved from 1820 and 1825 was a year of full employment and prosperity. However, it was followed, from 1827, by an economic depression. Whereas post-war distress was seen as the problem of adjusting to a peacetime economy, the recession of the late 1820s carried clear political implications for the new towns. An aristocratic government now seemed out of touch with the needs of an industrial economy. Thus, an economic problem was increasingly seen as requiring a political solution.

The death in 1827 of Lord Liverpool, Prime Minister and arch opponent of reform, seemed to open up the possibility of change. Nevertheless, attempts to use private members' bills in 1828 to disenfranchise the 'rotten' boroughs of Penryn and East Retford and to transfer their seats to Manchester and Birmingham failed. Clearly, the time had come for a more general measure that the government would sponsor and the House of Commons could support, and this point was increasingly accepted in the country as a whole. One notable exception to this feeling was the Duke of Wellington, who became Tory Prime Minister in 1828 but resigned in November 1830 following a hostile parliamentary response to his anti-reform speech (see page 20). The Whigs, in opposition almost continually since 1784, saw their opportunity to seize and retain power. Under the leadership of Earl Grey they formed a government and introduced a Reform Bill. This planned to redistribute the representation from a number of rotten boroughs, at the same time as introducing a uniform £10 householder franchise in all boroughs. By this, men who owned a house rated at the value of £10 a year and over would be able to vote. Grey was a wealthy landowner who, unlike Wellington, understood how widespread the call for reform had become. But there was a good deal of opposition from the Commons and Grey's bill passed its second reading in March 1831 by only one vote. Following this, Grey persuaded the king to dissolve Parliament so he might seek support from the country in a general election. The Whigs were re-elected, on a reform platform, by a large majority (by the standards of the day) of over 130 seats.

Grey felt he had received a mandate to re-introduce reform and a second Reform bill passed through the Commons in July. Yet it is worth bearing in mind that, however revolutionary and threatening the Whigs' proposals were seen to be within the landed classes, Grey had no wish to change the *status quo*. He wanted to use what was really a rather limited reform to reinforce the system rather than to change it fundamentally. Above all, the working-class voter was to be excluded. As he assured the House of Lords in November 1832: 'there is no one more decided against annual parliaments, universal suffrage, and vote by ballot, than I am. My object is not to favour, but to put an end to such hopes'.

b) The Campaign in the Country

Outside Parliament agitation for reform focused on the figure of Thomas Attwood, a Birmingham banker whose family fortune had been made in the Midlands iron trade. He had gained some attention as a currency reformer who believed that the decision to move the economy on to the Gold Standard in 1821 had been damaging. In an attempt to stop rising post-war prices, Lord Liverpool's government limited the issue of bank notes to the level of gold bullion held by the

Bank of England. Attwood took the opposite view, arguing that domestic demand could be stimulated by inflating the economy with paper money. By political inclination a Tory, he had taken no part in the post-war reform movement and was opposed to universal suffrage. However, Attwood attracted the support of men of his own class when he argued that the economy would continue to be unstable while the new industrial middle class was excluded from government.

In 1829 Attwood, and others, were struck by the success in Ireland of Daniel O'Connell in forcing Wellington's government to repeal the restrictions on Roman Catholics participating in British public affairs. Backed by his popular organisation, the Catholic Association, O'Connell, himself a Roman Catholic, had been elected MP for County Clare but was initially disbarred from taking his seat by virtue of his religion. Such was the intensity of the agitation orchestrated by the Catholic Association that Wellington, fearing civil war, gave way and supported Roman Catholic emancipation. For men like Attwood, previously fearful of harnessing popular support, O'Connell's success stressed the potential of a mass-based movement. Roman Catholic emancipation also split the Tories and opened the way for Grey's reform-minded government.

In 1830 Attwood formed the Birmingham Political Union (BPU) and modelled it closely on O'Connell's association. He planned a massive organisation in which a middle-class leadership and a working-class rank and file would be bound together by a common objective. The problem with Parliament, he argued, was the absence of men representing productive capital (men like Attwood in fact!). He stressed the common interests of the employers and employees who together made up a single 'productive class'. As he put it:

> The interests of masters and men are, in fact, one. If the masters flourish the men flourish with them; and if the masters suffer difficulties their difficulties must shortly affect the workmen in three-fold degree.

This was really only an extension of the idea of 'virtual representation'; in this case the interests of the employee would be represented by the employer. It was not always a very convincing argument. After all, if the economic interest of the two groups were so close, how does one explain the growth of aggressive trade unionism in the period? (See Chapters 3 and 4.) It is also important to note that Attwood did not come to reform from the Painite tradition previously outlined. For him universal suffrage was unnecessary. Given the common interests of employers and employees, the needs of the working community would be fully catered for if employers were returned to Parliament. For this reason the Political Council of the BPU consisted entirely of middle-class men. As Attwood said: 'Who would ever think ... of sending even a disciplined army into the field without officers?'

Despite this heavily qualified commitment to democracy on the part of its founder, the BPU was enormously popular, attracting strong working-class support. It regularly drew 50–100,000 people to its outdoor meetings and Attwood was a popular speaker on these occasions. Similar political unions were established in towns throughout the country, most significantly the Northern Political Union in Newcastle, and, in London, the National Political Union. The latter was organised by Francis Place, a tailor who had been active in the earlier period of radicalism and who now accepted the need to act with, in his words, men of 'money and influence'. These political unions now backed the Whig Bill which promised to disenfranchise the 'rotten' boroughs, give seats to the large towns and introduce a uniform, though property based, borough franchise. Yet, given the far wider nature of the earlier radical programme, why was there now so much working-class support for this rather limited proposal?

The earlier programme had not been forgotten. Throughout the campaign it was advocated by the London-based National Union of the Working Classes, formed in 1831. This organisation never attracted mass support but with its radical programme and a network of branches throughout the country it was an influential forerunner of Chartism. Through the medium of the illegal, but very popular, *Poor Man's Guardian* newspaper it expressed distrust for the Bill and its supporters, particularly Attwood. Yet, taken as a whole, working people do seem to have given the Bill genuine support. This partly reflected a belief that its enactment would be the initial step towards full democracy. This was certainly not in the minds of the men who framed the Bill. They sought a minimal adjustment to maintain the *status quo*. Yet at this stage gradual reform still seemed a viable alternative, especially given the failure of the earlier and more comprehensive programme. The lessons of 1815–20 had been learned, and the advantages of lining up behind men of wealth were recognised in the working community. As Bronterre O'Brien, editor of the *Poor Man's Guardian* and later to be a prominent Chartist leader, said of the Bill:

> ... with all its faults we are willing to receive it as an instalment or part payment of the debt of right due to us; for we feel assured that under its provisions, the electoral right will ultimately be capable of expanding and purifying itself into a perfect representative system.

A similar line was taken by the National Union of the Working Classes which maintained its commitment to universal manhood suffrage but still supported the Bill. The leader of the Manchester cotton spinners, John Doherty, editor of the working-class newspaper *The Voice of the People,* summed up the high hopes of the people he represented:

> The day is not far distant, when we shall assume our station in society, and when we shall no longer be called the 'rabble' or the 'swinish multitude' etc. etc. but will receive liberty and happiness.

However, the Act itself did not deliver those benefits, nor was it intended to by its originators in Parliament. It was from the betrayal of these hopes Chartism would grow in the 1830s.

For their part Attwood and his supporters recognised that the greater the numbers behind the political unions, the more they could claim to speak for the 'people' with all the authority this would suggest. Through 1831 and early 1832 the political unions called a series of public meetings to put pressure on Parliament to accept the Bill. The House of Commons, in particular, was influenced by such pressure. Here the opposition to the Bill was very fragmented. Robert Peel, who led the Tories in the Commons, certainly opposed the Bill as being too broad a measure, but he also rejected the traditional Toryism of the die-hard Ultra-Tories who would consider no reform at all. Peel did not accept that the unreformed system actually did exclude the new middle class. His own father had been a textile manufacturer who had entered Parliament by purchasing a seat. But he did accept that the system was now discredited and needed its worst excesses removed. Tory disunity in the Commons was to prove crucial to the Bill's success.

The House of Lords, where Wellington was the major influence, was a different matter. Made up largely of the county aristocracy it was less aware of, or concerned with, the agitation centred on the growing towns and industrial districts. The Bill was passed in the Commons in September 1831, but was rejected by the Lords in October.

The rejection gave rise to rioting in Nottingham, Derby and Bristol which had to be suppressed by troops. In November 1831 the BPU announced its intention to put itself on a military footing. A revised Bill, with a slightly more restrictive franchise, was now introduced. This was passed by the Commons the following March but it was feared that the Lords would reject it when they debated it in May 1832. The Cabinet now demanded that the King create new peers to ensure the Bill's passage. When he refused Grey resigned. It was now widely expected that the King would appoint Wellington who would block reform and arrest the leaders of the countrywide movement.

On 11 May 1832 representatives of the BPU and other political unions met with Francis Place in London to discuss their possible response to such a move. According to Place they considered non-payment of taxes, a run on the banks and armed resistance. In the tense days that followed, the BPU protected Attwood from possible arrest, with a bodyguard of 1,500 armed men. In the event, the Commons voted to support Grey's outgoing ministry, Wellington recognised that he could not form a viable government, and the King agreed to the creation of new peers. This proved unnecessary: under threat, the Lords capitulated and passed the Bill which then became law in June.

c) Revolution and the 'Days of May'

How close did Britain come to a revolution during the Reform Bill campaign? Historians are divided. E.P. Thompson claims that 'Britain was within an ace of revolution' and he identifies the autumn of 1831 with the riots that followed the Lords' rejection, and the Days of May 1832, as the potentially revolutionary moments. An alternative view, expressed most extensively by Joseph Hamburger in his book *James Mill and the Art of Revolution* (1963), claims that the middle-class reformers were engaged in an extravagant form of bluff. They played up the extent of national support and exaggerated its violent potential in an effort to force the Bill through a reluctant Parliament. There never was a real threat of revolution: 'The professional reformer like the public relations man', Hamburger claims, 'dealt in images'.

Elsewhere *(Politics and Production in the Early Nineteenth Century,* 1990), I have argued that far from massaging images and manipulating figures of attendance at reform meetings, the middle-class leaders of the campaign were 'riding the tiger' in relation to their working-class rank and file. That is to say, that they were operating on the back of forces that they might not always be able to control. As we have seen, the working community possessed by this time a tradition of political activity and also a political programme far more radical than that envisaged by men like Place and Attwood. The crucial problem for the middle-class radicals was not the creation of false images to frighten the government, but rather retaining the leadership of a mass-based movement and directing it towards a moderate reform of Parliament. Riding the tiger is an exhilarating activity, but the rider is never totally in charge since the tiger has a mind of its own and can turn.

This is not to deny that bluff figured somewhere in the reformers' calculations. Attwood frequently referred to the tactics of 'wholesome terror' whereby the peaceful process of petitioning Parliament was backed by the rhetoric of violent language. An example of what might be called the 'language of menace' was given by Attwood at a mass rally outside Birmingham in May 1832. Attwood told the estimated 200,000-strong crowd:

> I would rather die than see the great Bill of reform rejected or muti-
> lated. I see that you are all of one mind on the subject ... Answer me
> then, had you not all rather die than live the slaves of the borough-
> mongers? (All! All!)

Such oratory was calculated to have its impact not only upon the audience, but also upon those in authority. There had been another revolution in France in 1830 and memories of the post-war radical movement were still relatively fresh. When the BPU published its plan to arm in November 1831, the King wrote to Wellington that he feared a revolutionary intent on the Union's part. However, we must remember that this was primarily a peaceful movement to petition Parliament in support of a limited reform measure which had been proposed by the government of the day and had been accepted by the Commons. Attwood, for example, was happy to drop the plan to arm the BPU when the Whigs put it to him that its illegality would reduce the support for the Bill in the Commons. There was a very clear element of platform posturing and display by the middle-class leaders of the reform movement.

Any revolutionary threat came not from the conscious intent of the reformers, but from the circumstances of the moment, and these were, in many ways, beyond their control. Above all, this was the only time in British history when the working class and the middle class were firmly united in an extra-parliamentary campaign for political reform. This had not been the case in the post-war period, nor would it be in Chartism. By May 1832 the movement covered a broad social spectrum. Support ranged from wealthy industrialists, professionals and merchants, who simply sought an adjustment in the political system to allow in the urban interest via a restricted property franchise, right through to the labouring poor who saw the Bill as the first step towards full citizenship. The wealth of an excluded middle class, backed by the numerical strength of an excluded working class, faced the intransigence of the House of Lords at this point.

At the same time, of course, working-class reformers within this fragile alliance carried with them the radical reform programme evolved in the post-war years. They also remembered from this period what might be expected from an anti-reform Tory administration. Had Wellington become Prime Minister in May 1832 and moved against the reformers it is difficult to see how bloodshed could have been avoided. The Duke's decision to stand down actually had more to do with the Commons' support for the Whigs than the clamour of the reform movement. Nevertheless, the riots of October 1831 gave a fairly good insight into the feelings of the country. In April 1832 the universal suffrage paper, the *Poor Man's Guardian,* published Macerone's *Defensive Instructions for the People.* This guide to street-fighting by an Italian political refugee included 'do-it-yourself' plans for the construction of home-made pikes and a guide to their use. Such advice, the paper noted, might be acted upon were the 'people' attacked.

Thus revolution was more likely to be precipitated by an injudicious act by Wellington, had he become Prime Minister in May 1832, than by the conscious intent of reformers like Place and Attwood. This point is made by David Moss in his book *Thomas Attwood: The Biography of a Radical* (McGill-Queens University Press, 1990, p 221):

1 Attwood was the reverse of a revolutionary conspirator ... Everything
was still being conducted in the open to gain the maximum publicity.
Attwood had no wish to destroy the system. If he had been forced to
mobilise his followers, their chances against a determined government
5 would have been slight and he knew it ... The threat, however, had to
be made, in order to raise the spectre of British troops firing on the
British people ... [But] If Wellington had persisted and had proceeded
against the unions, Attwood would have been pushed into a difficult
position. At that stage he could not have backed down.

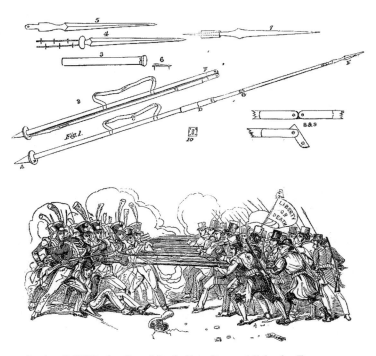

In April 1832, the *Poor Man's Guardian* published a European
revolutionary's guide to insurrection. In effect this illustration describes the
construction and use of home-made pikes. It is worth considering the
impact of this on the general sense of alarm during the 'Days of May'.

4 The Reform Act and its Significance

> **KEY ISSUE** Why were working-class radicals so disappointed with the results of the Reform Act?

The intransigence of the Lords converted the Reform Act into an heroic measure, an image which it would scarcely have sustained on its own merits. Its passing did little to dismantle the system which Burke had defended so fiercely in 1790, since it accepted the principle that the franchise should still be based on property ownership. Fifty-five boroughs with fewer than 2,000 inhabitants were disenfranchised and lost both MPs, whilst 33 boroughs with fewer than 4,000 inhabitants lost one of their MPs. This released 143 seats for re-distribution and mostly they were assigned to the industrial towns. Five new seats were given to Ireland, eight to Scotland and four to Wales. In the boroughs the older franchises were replaced by the £10 householder franchise. By this provision all male resident ratepaying householders, whose houses were valued, for the purposes of levying rates, at £10 per year or over were given the vote. This was actually more restrictive than it sounds. In England and Wales 1 man in 5 now had the vote, in Scotland 1 man in 8, in Ireland 1 man in 20. In Birmingham, for example, some 4,000 men were entitled to vote from a total population of around 144,000 in the new borough. Women were still excluded. Voting remained open and most elections continued to be uncontested (there were no contests in three-fifths of constituencies in the 1847 election, for example). The majority of MPs continued to come from landed backgrounds. Yet the urban middle-class interest had been admitted to political life and their presence would be felt increasingly in the years to come.

For working people there was only disappointment. The new House of Commons, elected in 1832, looked very much like the old institution and acted in fairly familiar ways. When rioting had broken out in the agricultural areas of the South in 1830 the 'reforming' Whigs, then in power, had suppressed it ruthlessly. They were as much a party of landowners as the Tories and the 'Captain Swing' disturbances, provoked by the use of threshing machinery in areas of high rural unemployment, had disturbed them considerably. The 'Swing' riots, so called because of their mythical leader, were really a series of small, unco-ordinated outbreaks (there was no 'Captain Swing) which reflected the farm labourers' concerns about changes in employment structures. The Whigs reacted as a party of landowners.

After the Reform Act, it was a Whig ministry which extended the State's arbitrary power in Ireland by the Irish Coercion Act of 1833. Trade unions were the subject of repression in 1834 and the Poor Law Amendment Act of the same year introduced a harsh new relief system. The Municipal Corporations Act of 1835 established town councils on a restricted property franchise. Excluded from national politics, the working community was also, by this measure, to be excluded from local politics. The record of Grey's 'reform' administration, and that of Melbourne who succeeded him in 1834, rather emphasised that working-class hopes for gradual reform were mistaken.

The Reform Act left a legacy of bitterness, and working-class euphoria at its passing did not last long. This sense of frustration and betrayal, which set in after 1832, took working-class reformers back to their earlier political programme of reform and this was now expressed in Chartism.

Summary Diagram
The Reform Act and Before: Reform Movements 1815–32

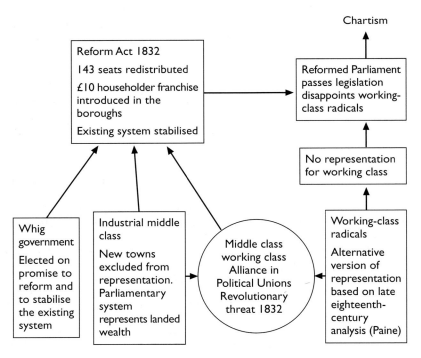

Working on Chapter 2

Understanding the contents of this chapter will be the key to a full analysis of the Chartist movement, which will be dealt with in the next chapter. You will need to go back over this chapter, making notes as you go, to ensure that you are able to explain the following:

(i) *the nature of the existing Parliamentary system before reform and the way it was defended;* this is vital to understanding why a political system that looks so indefensible to us today was actually so resilient;

(ii) *the criticisms of the system as expressed by the radicals;* this alternative view of politics formed the basis of Chartist beliefs and language in the 1830s and 1840s, so it is important to get the late eighteenth-century perspective straight in your mind;

(iii) *why the Reform Act was successfully passed when earlier reform initiatives had failed;* for all the faults of the Act, radicals felt that their pressure had pushed the Bill through Parliament. The Reform Bill campaign now became the model of a constitutional mass movement and this is vital to an understanding of the strategies subsequently adopted by the Chartists.

One important point to bear in mind with all of these questions is that there were a range of approaches to reform available at the time, drawing on diverse social perspectives and often very different views on the nature of representative government. Take some of the characters and look at what they are quoted as having said about reform in the chapter.

• Duke of Wellington (a Tory aristocrat) page 20
• Sir Robert Peel (a self-made Tory politician with a family background in trade) page 29
• Earl Grey (Prime Minister and a Whig aristocrat) page 26
• Thomas Attwood (an industrialist-banker from the new middle class) page 27
• Bronterre O'Brien (a radical journalist and a Painite, later to be a Chartist leader) page 28
• John Doherty (a trade unionist) page 28

They each looked at reform from a different point of view. So, by way of general preparation for tackling essays of this sort, ask yourself *'What was wrong with parliamentary representation in 1830?'* and try to answer it from the point of view of each of these individuals. This exercise in *empathy* will give you a good insight into why so much of British society seemed to be moving in the same direction (though for different reasons) during the Reform Bill agitation. It will also provide a way into an understanding of the wider context.

Answering structured and essay questions on Chapter 2

Sometimes essay questions will be presented in two or three interrelated parts (sometimes called a 'stepped question'). Generally, the first two parts will ask you to focus on the identification of key issues or individuals whilst the third part will focus more fully on the analysis of causation. For example;

a) What was wrong with the electoral system before 1832? (*5 marks*)
b) What did Thomas Attwood contribute to the movement for reform during the period 1830–1832? (*5 marks*)
c) Does the Reform Act of 1832 deserve to be described as 'Great'? (*10 marks*)

In a) you will need to explain why the political system was so unsatisfactory to so many different social groups at the time (with detailed examples of the sort provided in the chapter). In b) you will need to explain who Attwood was and his view of why the political system was unresponsive to the needs of the new middle class. You then need to link this to the agitation for reform outside Parliament, which Attwood orchestrated. Part c) asks if the Reform Act deserves its common descriptor of 'Great'. The exercise in the 'Working on' section above will be particularly useful in answering this question. Ask yourself which of the characters listed in the exercise might have seen the Act as deserving of the title 'Great' and which might have had doubts, and think of them as representatives of particular social groups. What was the motivation of the Whigs in introducing the Act into Parliament? Also, how does the Act look to us in retrospect, in terms of the development of a representative system?

Essay questions on this subject often revolve around the issue of where the pressures for reform were located in this period. Thus, the challenge of this sort of question lies in identifying a range of contributory factors and assessing their relative significance. Here are some examples:

1. What pressures brought about the reform of Parliament in 1832?
2. Why were its opponents unable to prevent the passing of the Parliamentary Reform Act in 1832?
3. What were the main causes of discontent between 1815 and 1832?
4. How close did Britain come to a revolution in the reform crisis of 1832 and why was any danger averted?
5. What part was played by economic depression in stimulating radical politics between 1815 and 1850?

Questions 1 to 3 are good examples of the kind of questions where you are left with a fairly free hand to arrange the contributory factors into the kind of order that you feel makes the most convincing explanation. Question 5 presents you with one factor, economic depression, and asks you to judge its relative importance (this time across a wider time-scale). Question 4 raises the popular issue of the extent to which the pressure for reform created a revolutionary situation. Your answers to each of these questions will need to take some account of economic change, the emergence of new social groups, the state of flux in party politics, the growth of a reform movement in the country and the opposition to reform. In questions 1, 2 and 4 you will need to analyse the underlying nature of the agitation and the strategies adopted to put pressure on Parliament to change the electoral system. This could be developed in each question by a detailed analysis of the 'Days of May'.

Source-based questions on Chapter 2

1. Approaches to representation

1. Read Edmund Burke's statements on the unreformed House of Commons (pages 19 and 21). Answer the following questions:
   a) What does he mean by the phrase, 'without shutting its doors to any merit in any class'? (*2 marks*)
   b) Which groups are left out of this list of what is included in the House of Commons? (*2 marks*)
   c) How could Burke justify his view that the House of Commons was a representative institution? (*2 marks*)
   d) Using your knowledge gained from the chapter, explain why Burke's view may have become controversial in the period after 1815. (*5 marks*).

2. Compare the the statements by Earl Grey, Bronterre O'Brien and John Doherty on the Reform Bill (pages 26 and 28). Using the knowledge you have gained from reading the chapter, answer the following questions:
   a) What does Grey mean when he says the Reform Bill would 'Put an end to such hopes.'? (*2 marks*)
   b) What does O'Brien mean by 'the debt of right due to us'? (*2 marks*)
   c) What does Doherty hope for from the Reform Act? (*2 marks*)
   d) Where does the term 'swinish multitude' originate from? (*2 marks*)
   e) Using the knowledge you have gained from reading this chapter, explain why those radicals whose ultimate goal was universal suffrage were always going to be disappointed by the Reform Act. (*8 marks*)

3 Chartism

POINTS TO CONSIDER

This chapter explores the emergence of Chartism from the discontent of the 1830s, the structure of the movement, and the reasons for its failure. It focuses on how we interpret the movement and its leadership. Above all it seeks to view the Chartists in their own terms and to see the movement as they would have seen it. This will involve you in confronting some assumptions about the nature and capabilities of the working community at the time.

KEY DATES

1833 Formation of the Grand National Consolidated Trades' Union Factory Act reduces hours for children in textile mills, but not for adults; leads to formation of Short time Committees.

1834 Tolpuddle case, six Dorchester labourers transported for joining the GNCTU; New Poor Law passed. It appears to criminalise poverty by aiming to make the Workhouse the only poor relief available.

1836 Taxes on newspapers lowered.

1837 New Poor Law applied in the Midlands and the North gives rise to extensive opposition.

1838 People's Charter published and incorporated into a National Petition.

1839 February, Chartist Convention meets in London; July, first petition rejected; July, Bull Ring riots in Birmingham; November, Newport Uprising.

1840 Formation of the National Charter Association.

1841 Chartist church established.

1842 Rejection of the second petition; Formation of the Complete Suffrage Union; August, Plug disturbances.

1845 Formation of the Chartist Land Company.

1848 April, rejection of the third petition.

1855 Death of Feargus O'Connor.

There can be little doubt that Chartism was the most extensive British radical movement of the nineteenth century. It aimed to achieve political rights for working men and can be said to have run from, roughly, 1838 to 1858. The degree of support that it engendered varied greatly within this 20-year period. Enthusiasm was at its height on the submission of the three Chartist petitions to Parliament in 1839, 1842 and 1848. After 1848 Chartism faded to a minority movement of small political clubs, and government fears of potential unrest finally subsided. Yet at the height of its powers Chartism commanded extensive support from the working community, which would have been the main beneficiary of its proposed reforms.

These reforms were contained in a six-point programme, the People's Charter, which demanded: 1. universal manhood suffrage; 2. the secret ballot; 3. annual parliaments; 4. the creation of electoral districts of equal size so that representation would be spread evenly throughout the country; 5. the payment of wages to MPs; and 6. the abolition of the property qualification for MPs, so that people without property could stand for Parliament. Under these provisions working men would have been able to participate in politics as both voters and representatives, within a democratic process that was constantly in motion as a result of annual parliaments. The Chartist version of democracy put great emphasis on the maintenance of real contact between the governors and the governed.

The 'six points' were embodied in the three Chartist petitions, each of which was rejected in Parliament by a huge majority. Despite its massive following Chartism was unsuccessful in achieving any of its six aims during the period of its existence. The fact that by 1918 all of these demands, with the exception of annual parliaments, would be implemented in full could obviously do nothing to offset the Chartists' own sense of failure. Looking back from our own political system the demands seem, in themselves, eminently reasonable. After all, today we all exercise most of the rights the Chartists demanded. Given this, Chartism really poses three major questions for historians: why did it emerge when it did? what was its exact nature? and, above all, why did it fail?

1 The Emergence of Chartism

> **KEY ISSUE** Chartism is sometimes described as an 'umbrella movement' gathering under its shelter a range of earlier movements. What did Chartism draw from these earlier movements?

Chartism can be seen to have grown from the failure of the Reform Act of 1832 to deliver a radically reformed political system. Thomas Attwood, as a newly elected member for Birmingham, found himself one of a small minority of middle-class MPs in a still predominantly landed House of Commons, where Members sniggered at his Midlands accent whenever he spoke. Like many other middle-class men he now argued that all male householders who owned a house and paid rates on it should be given the vote (household suffrage). Of course, even this measure would still have excluded most working men from the franchise.

For their part, disillusionment with the Reform Act led working-class radicals to seek alternative ways of dealing with the many problems of life in an industrial society. The period between 1832 and 1838 saw the development of socialist responses and the flourishing of trade unions. Alongside this, major campaigns took place against newspaper taxes, the factory system, and the New Poor Law. Each of these contributed, in different ways, to the nature of the Chartist movement that followed.

a) Socialism and the Growth of the Trade Unions

By the 1830s working people looked at industrial society and asked themselves two related questions. First, given that the workforce, through its daily labour, created the new wealth, why did it receive so little of it in return? At exactly the point where the nation was increasing its wealth, working people found themselves clinging precariously to subsistence. Secondly, why was it that in a period of 'labour saving' inventions and techniques, work seemed to be getting harder? Answers to these questions were being developed, in the 1820s and 1830s, by a group of early socialist thinkers, the most prominent of whom was Robert Owen. For this reason these answers are often referred to collectively as 'Owenism'.

Owen was a wealthy Welshman who owned and ran a cotton mill in New Lanark, Scotland, from 1799 until 1829. Here he took the unusual step of creating a community around the mill and encouraging his workers to increase production by incentives and involvement rather than by threats and punishments. He was motivated in this by his belief that 'a man's character is formed for him not by him'. If people lived in good conditions, he believed, they would become good people, whilst bad conditions would lead people to behave badly. This was a very optimistic philosophy which rejected the traditional Christian ideal that human nature was inherently sinful. Instead, Owen accepted the late eighteenth-century belief in the 'perfectability of man' given the right material and moral environment in which to thrive. The problem with industrial society, Owen argued, lay in its essentially competitive nature. How much better it would be to base a society on the same ethos of co-operation that he had established among his workers at New Lanark. To this end, between 1821 and 1843, he was involved in establishing six self-sufficient communities in Britain (and one in the United States) based upon the principle of co-operation. Here working people tried to meet their own needs communally, growing their own food, producing their own goods, sharing their resources and providing their own education and culture. None of these ideal communities was in existence for very long and they served to emphasise the difficulties of establishing socialist communities within a competitive industrial society. Nevertheless, the idea that there might be an alternative way of organising society and distributing its rewards captured the imagination of many working-class radicals. Other co-operative schemes were floated in these years. By 1832 about 500 local co-operative societies had established shops which shared their profits with their customers. Originally designed to fund the establishment of communities, the shops swiftly became an end in themselves. In London, Birmingham, Manchester and Leeds, plans were set in train to open Labour Exchange Bazaars which used a currency based on labour hours. Here a shoemaker, for example, might exchange a pair of shoes he had made for a labour note which reflected the labour time that was adjudged to have gone into their production (see illustration). This could then be spent on any other goods on display in the Bazaar, which would all be priced in terms of hours. This novel scheme soon failed; only two Exchanges were ever opened, one in London in September 1832, and the other in Birmingham in 1833. By early 1834 both had closed. Workers needed to exchange the goods they produced for foodstuffs rather than for the various forms of industrial produce that accumulated in the Exchanges.

The disappointments of political agitation in 1832, and the improvement in trade from 1833, led many to turn to trade unions whose legality had been re-instated with the repeal of the Combination Acts in 1824. There were many strikes in these years but the unions were mostly highly fragmented, locally based, organisations of single trades. Owen was persuaded in 1833 by a number of his working-class followers that the formation of a massive union of men and women from every trade, based on co-operative principles, could peacefully transform society. But Owen was never very enthusiastic in his support for the resulting Grand National Consolidated

Owenite labour note, 1833. This note was produced by the Birmingham Labour Exchange for use as currency within the scheme.

Trades' Union (GNCTU), formed in February 1834. As an ex-employer he felt unions were vehicles for the kind of class conflict he wished to avoid. Yet even he was drawn to the idea of a general union that would include employers in its ranks and which aimed to achieve success by persuasion rather than coercion, as Owen himself had done at New Lanark.

The idea of a general union was not new. John Gast, a London shipwright, had formed one in 1818 called the 'Philanthropic Hercules', but it only ran for a few months. John Doherty, the Manchester spinners' leader, was more successful in a similar venture: his National Association for the Protection of Labour ran from 1829 until 1832 and achieved a membership of somewhere between 60,000 and 80,000 members. Although the GNCTU never grew to this size – it attracted no more than 16,000 members – it did draw the attention of the Whig government which was fearful of its potential appeal. Unions conventionally brought together workers in one area or one trade, and these were considered enough of a threat to have been made illegal in 1799 and 1800 by the Combination Acts. Unions that drew support from a variety of trades were even more threatening because they aimed to speak for a whole class rather than just a trade.

By July 1834 the GNCTU was dead, victim of the government's war against the unions, declared with the arrest of six farm labourers from Tolpuddle in Dorset. Their crime was to have sworn an illegal oath during a trade union initiation ceremony. For a government of landowners, mindful of the recent 'Swing' disturbances in the rural areas of the south, this seemed an appropriate moment to deal with the unions. The GNCTU took up the cause of the 'Tolpuddle martyrs' and organised a mass meeting of 35,000 people, in Copenhagen Fields, London, to call for their release. But the sentences of seven years' transportation meted out to George Loveless and his five Tolpuddle companions dealt a blow from which the GNCTU simply never recovered. Even under the Combination Acts the maximum sentence had been three months' imprisonment. To deal with a union movement that seemed to be growing, the Whigs revived a piece of legislation passed in 1797 to discourage naval mutinies and it was under this that the Dorset men were convicted. After 1834 trade unions continued as organisations of particular trades in local areas; but for the moment this was the end of schemes to draw them together, nationally, from across the trades.

In fact, all of the Owenite schemes failed in the long or short term, so what was the lasting impact of Owenism? Historians have traditionally been rather hard on the Owenites, condemning their schemes as absurd or, at best, naive. However, what must be remembered with all early nineteenth-century radical movements (including Chartism) is that industrialisation was still in its formative stages. At this point it must have seemed as if its direction and form could have been changed dramatically by firm radical initiatives. The fact that we can look back and argue that the Labour Exchanges or the communities were bound to fail does not help us to recapture the hopes and aspirations of the men and women who took part in the schemes. Many carried their enthusiasm for a more equitable society into more overtly political movements. A large number of those who became involved in Chartism in 1838 had earlier been part of the Owenite movement. William Lovett, the London cabinet-maker and secretary to the first Chartist Convention, or Bronterre O'Brien, the 'Schoolmaster of Chartism' as he became known, are just two examples from the national leadership of the movement.

b) The War of the Unstamped

After the Reform Act an illegal newspaper press continued to push for further reform. In response the Whigs moved against the radical journalists and publishers with the same ferocity that they employed against the 'Swing' rioters in 1831 and the trade unionists in 1834. As a result the freedom of the press became an issue in itself.

Under the Six Acts of 1819 a newspaper was considered to be any publication carrying news and appearing at less than 26-day intervals. A newspaper had to carry a government stamp and sell for at least 7d. Failure to carry a stamp made the publication illegal. The stamp duties were intended to reduce the working-class readership of radical papers by keeping their prices high. As always, however, there were ways around the law. John Gast published a successful trade union paper in London called the *Trades' Newspaper* between 1825 and 1828. This carried a government stamp and sold at 7d, but union branches clubbed together to buy shares in the paper. Each branch would take one copy of the paper and have it read aloud at meetings. Radical journalist William Carpenter published a newspaper called the *Political Letter*. This took the form of an open letter to a leading public figure: Carpenter would choose a different one each week. Although his paper contained news, he argued that it was really a letter and thus not covered by the 1819 legislation. The courts disagreed and imprisoned him in 1831. Some publishers even printed on cloth, arguing that their publications could not therefore be considered *newspapers*.

But in 1831, as the Reform Bill campaign reached its height, the London printer Henry Hetherington decided to dispense with such subtleties. Hetherington, a supporter of universal suffrage and at one time a follower of Owen, started the *Poor Man's Guardian* as a penny newspaper. This appeared each week under the explicit heading:

Published contrary to 'law' to try the power of 'might' against 'right'

The paper claimed that the newspaper stamp was a tax on knowledge. It also carried the significant motto, 'Knowledge is power'.

The *Poor Man's Guardian* ran in this overtly illegal way from 1831 to

1835. It proved enormously popular, with a circulation of about 16,000 copies at its height. As with all radical journals its actual readership was much greater than its sales. It would be passed around from one reader to another or read aloud to groups. We may need to multiply sales figures by ten to arrive at the total of actual readers. Its success also encouraged a host of other unstamped papers to appear in both London and the provinces. These continued to appear despite the prosecutions of many of those who published and sold them. Hetherington was himself imprisoned twice but the *Guardian* continued to appear on the streets. In London alone 740 vendors of the unstamped were brought to trial between 1831 and 1836. Eventually, the Whig government of Lord Melbourne gave in and, in 1836, lowered the tax to a point where newspapers retailed at 4d.

The lowering of the 'taxes on knowledge' showed that determined pressure could move governments. It also meant that the later Chartist papers, like the *Northern Star,* could appear as legal publications selling at a lower price. The government stamp that the *Star* bore even entitled it to the benefit of free delivery by the Post Office! Chartism appeared at a time when the press was freer than it had ever been before, as a result of the efforts of men like Hetherington.

Like the Owenite organisations, the 'War of the Unstamped' was a training ground for the later Chartist leadership. Bronterre O'Brien, for example, edited the *Poor Man's Guardian* from 1832. George Julian Harney, who edited the *Northern Star* from 1845, served his radical apprenticeship as a shop-boy for Hetherington. Above all, the popularity of universal suffrage papers like the *Guardian* demonstrated the continued enthusiasm that existed in the working community for further parliamentary reform.

c) Opposition to the Factory and the New Poor Law

During the 1830s the concerns of the working community of the rapidly developing industrial areas of Lancashire and Yorkshire were expressed most clearly in campaigns against the factory system and, after 1837, against the New Poor Law. Although the factory was an important part of industrialisation, it was really only the spinning processes involved in the Lancashire cotton industry and the woollen trades of the West Riding of Yorkshire that had been fully adapted to factory production by this time. Working people entered the factory reluctantly, preferring the greater control of work and their own time that the domestic system of home working allowed. Factory hours were long and monotonous, whereas in the home work could proceed at the family's own pace. Factory workers in both of these areas formed Short Time Committees to call on Parliament to pass an act that would limit the hours of work for all operatives to ten per day. John Doherty, the spinners' leader, played a prominent part in this campaign which also attracted support from outside the working class.

In Yorkshire Richard Oastler took up the cause of child workers in the factories. Oastler was the steward of a large landed estate just outside Huddersfield. The estate was owned by an absentee landlord and, in his absence, Oastler acted the part of a landowner. For him the exploitation of small children as factory labour epitomised the uncaring nature of the new industrial society. He argued that before the Industrial Revolution a landowner looked after his tenants and employees as a father would his family. With industrialisation this paternalism was replaced by a system in which employers accepted no obligations to their employees beyond the payment of wages for work done. Politically Oastler was a Tory. His motto of 'Altar, Throne, and Cottage' stressed his commitment to those traditional values which industrial change appeared to threaten. His belief in the importance of wealth playing a guiding role led him to oppose universal suffrage as both unnecessary and undesirable. Yet his energetic championing of factory reform gave him a huge popularity with working people, who called him 'King of the Factory Children'. This was partly because his view of industrialisation rather reflected that of the working-class radicals, who agreed that both the quality of social relationships and the standard of living had been better in the period before the Industrial Revolution. So Oastler's view that universal suffrage would result in 'universal confusion' did not, at this stage, detract from the rapport that he was able to establish with the Short Time Committees.

Also prominent in the agitation was John Fielden, the owner of a large cotton spinning factory in Lancashire. A supporter of universal suffrage and MP for Oldham from 1832, he was appalled to discover in 1835 that the small children in his own factory walked a full 20 miles in their 12-hour shift. Needless to say, Fielden's political views were unusual for a man of his class. Yet he was to remain an active supporter of working-class movements throughout his parliamentary career.

Large public meetings in favour of factory reform, at which Oastler was a favourite speaker, forced the Whig government to take the issue seriously. The resulting Factory Act of 1833 disappointed campaigners as it only limited the hours worked by children, leaving adult hours untouched. It was not until 1847 that a Ten Hours Act was passed.

Although the Short Time Committees continued to agitate, after 1833 they despaired of success. They turned their attentions to orchestrating opposition to the New Poor Law. By the end of 1836 the Poor Law Amendment Act had been extensively applied in the south of the country. The Poor Law Commissioners, led by Alfred Power, now turned their attention to the North, the Midlands, and Wales. Power was a barrister and had assisted in drafting the Act of 1834. He had also been part of the Royal Commission whose report into factory conditions had led to the inadequacies of the 1833 Factory Act. He was not a popular man in the North.

Nor was the New Poor Law popular. Parliament had been appalled at the rising cost of poor relief, and in 1832 appointed a Royal

Commission to recommend changes in the administration of the Poor Laws in England and Wales. This enquiry was led by Edwin Chadwick, a disciple of Jeremy Bentham, the political philosopher. Bentham (who died in 1832) argued that in general the government should not take an interventionist role in the social and economic life of the country. If individuals were left to pursue their own best interests, investing their capital in a truly free market, the economy would flourish and living standards would rise. Indeed, unwarranted interference by the state might well upset this delicate market mechanism. Nevertheless, Bentham argued, exceptionally the government would simply have to intervene to offset some of the worst problems caused by industrialisation; perhaps in the fields of public health, crime prevention or education. He thus established the idea of 'rule and exception' in social policy; as a rule the state would not intervene but exceptionally it might have to. Following this free-market principle, Chadwick's enquiry found that the cause of poverty lay in overexcessive intervention by the authorities in the form of poor relief. The Old Poor Law, administered under Tudor legislation, was considered to be actively encouraging the able-bodied poor to live on poor relief rather than seeking employment. His Report, published in 1834, celebrated this 'discovery':

> One of the most encouraging of the results of our enquiry is the degree to which the existing pauperism arises from fraud, indolence, and improvidence.

Chadwick's answer was to abolish the giving of poor relief in the form of either cash or food at the pauper's own home (out-relief). In future relief would only be available in the workhouse (in-relief). To encourage the able-bodied not to apply, the conditions in the workhouses would be worse (or as it was put 'less eligible') than the worst conditions endured, outside the workhouse, by those in employment. Given the dreadful living conditions in the towns, Chadwick had clearly set the workhouse masters a real problem in applying the principle of 'less eligibility'. How could worse conditions than these be created whilst also meeting the paupers' basic need for food and shelter? In fact, less eligibility was generally achieved not by short rations, as a reader of *Oliver Twist* might imagine, but rather by a series of psychological devices. Workhouse inmates wore prison-style uniforms, families were divided with men in one part of the house and women in another, children were kept separate from parents, silence was enforced at meal times, hard labour was introduced, and so on.

When the Commissioners attempted to apply this system in the Midlands and the North in 1837 they were met by a wave of popular resentment. In Lancashire and Yorkshire the Short Time Committees transformed themselves into Anti-Poor Law Associations. By the start of the year Britain was entering a period of severe depression that would last, to a greater or lesser extent, until the end of 1842.

Woollen textiles were particularly badly hit in 1837. With mass unemployment in the West Riding, the idea that poverty was a self-inflicted wound for which the poor should be punished looked like, and was taken as, a calculated insult to the jobless.

The anger induced by such treatment was perhaps most clearly expressed by the Reverend J.R. Stephens, the movement's leading advocate in Lancashire. Stephens had been expelled from the Methodists for his political activities so he ran an independent chapel in Ashton-under-Lyne. Like Oastler (who was also prominent in this campaign), Stephens was a Tory-radical and rejected universal suffrage. But he saw the repeal of the Old Poor Law as the wealthy rejecting their moral obligation to support the poor. His 'hellfire and damnation' oratory drew its inspiration from the Old Testament and was much in demand from audiences at anti-Poor Law meetings. In a typical piece of invective, he told a meeting in Glasgow in 1838,

> If they will not reform this, aye uproot it all, they shall have the revolution they so much dread. We shall destroy their abodes of guilt, which they have reared to violate all law and God's book.

The workhouses were popularly referred to as 'Bastilles'. Like the French prison, the workhouse became the symbol of oppression and the object of popular attack. Wherever Commissioner Power appeared in the North he was met by demonstrations and riots. At Keighley in March 1837 a crowd tore the coat from his back. A similar response faced Commissioners attempting to apply the law in Wales.

The campaign against the New Poor Law also introduced the figure of Feargus O'Connor to the working class. O'Connor was the son of a wealthy protestant Irish landed family. He was trained in law and represented County Cork as an MP from 1832 until 1835. Originally he was a follower of O'Connell, but he broke with him when the architect of Catholic Emancipation agreed in 1835 to support the Whig government in Parliament. O'Connor moved to Leeds in 1837 and started the *Northern Star* as part of the agitation against the New Poor Law. He became the leading radical figure of his day and was perhaps most celebrated as a powerful and charismatic platform orator.

Little of this opposition to the New Poor Law was ultimately effective in the sense that the Act had been applied in most areas by the early 1840s. Instead, the energies of the anti-Poor Law campaigners were now transferred to the emerging Chartist movement. In 1838, as the economic crisis deepened, John Fielden's parliamentary motion for the repeal of the 1834 Act was rejected by a derisory 309 votes to 17. This made the point clearly that little would be achieved without first reforming the system of political representation. Significantly, 14 of the 20 Northern delegates to the first Chartist Convention in 1839 had been active in the fight against the New Poor

Law and the repeal of the measure became an important plank in the Chartist platform.

In their different ways each of these movements in the 1830s encouraged the growth of Chartism. The failure of the general unions, and the other Owenite schemes, suggested that it was the political arena that really counted. Success in the 'War of the Unstamped' showed that defiant persistence could gain results. But the campaigns against the factory and the New Poor Law demonstrated just what a prolonged process it would be to erode the 1832 settlement issue by issue. What seemed to be needed was a comprehensive reform of Parliament before dealing with these individual concerns. For this reason Chartism is sometimes seen as an 'umbrella' movement, gathering under its comprehensive political programme the radical issues of these earlier campaigns and drawing on the organisational experience of their leaders.

2 Chartism: The Nature of the Movement

> **KEY ISSUES** What kind of movement was Chartism, what were its underlying ideas, and what reaction did it engender from the authorities?

a) The Launching of Chartism

The 'People's Charter', containing the six points of parliamentary reform, was published in May 1838 by the London Working Men's Association, which had been formed two years earlier. William Lovett, secretary of the LWMA, worked with Francis Place and the radical MP Joseph Roebuck in writing the Charter. It was intended to provide the basis for an Act of Parliament. The Charter was adopted with enthusiasm in the North where the campaign against the New Poor Law had achieved great popular support but little parliamentary response. The moment seemed right to initiate a mass agitation in the style of the Reform Bill campaign.

Indeed, the Birmingham Political Union had itself been re-formed in April 1837. But this time working people refused to join it in any numbers, deterred by Attwood's advocacy of household, rather than universal manhood, suffrage. However, in January 1838 Attwood announced a personal change of heart. 'I am a thorough convert to universal suffrage', he explained, 'and if ever I uttered a word against it I now altogether retract it'. This belated, and it should be said rather reluctant, adhesion to the first principle of the Charter was the price Attwood had to pay to allay working-class distrust created by their disappointment with the Reform Act. After the experience of 1832 a gradualist reform strategy was no longer credible as far as working-class radicals were concerned. But, with Attwood's change of heart, working people flocked to join the BPU in the early months of 1838. Its Political Council, which still consisted entirely of middle-class men, came up with the idea of a national petition for parliamentary reform, rather than the series of local petitions that had been tried in earlier campaigns.

Representatives of the LWMA, the BPU, and also Northern activists like O'Connor, fresh from their battles over the Poor Law, came together at a public meeting in Glasgow in May 1838. This venue was chosen deliberately. Five leading members of the town's cotton spinners' trade union had just been sentenced to seven years' transportation for conspiracy, administering illegal oaths and conducting union business in secret. A more serious charge of murder was found not proven. The case grew out of a prolonged strike against wage reductions in 1837. The similarities with the Tolpuddle affair were strong, and this was fresh in the public mind. After a lengthy campaign the six Dorset men had been given free pardons, and had arrived back from Australia in June 1837 to much acclaim. The Glasgow case appeared to be a renewed attack on the unions. Taken alongside the New Poor Law there seemed to be a calculated policy, on the part of the Whig government, to undermine both workplace organisations and the 'right' to out-relief – two crucial aspects of working-class life.

The Glasgow meeting drew 150,000 people. Here the idea of convening a Convention was floated. Delegates to the Chartist Convention would be elected at public meetings throughout the country. They would then be responsible for collecting signatures in their areas for a national petition along the lines suggested by the BPU. This petition would incorporate the Charter with its six points. The Convention would then meet to organise the presentation of the petition to Parliament.

Chartism grew, as an organisation, directly from the demonstration in Glasgow. It is significant that it should have emerged from a meeting called to protest at the government's treatment of trade unions and its poor relief legislation. The way the movement came about tells us a good deal about its nature. Chartism was never narrowly political in its outlook. Its politics were related to issues of direct concern to the working community.

In the summer of 1838 the work of organisation continued. The Great Northern Union was formed in June, based at Leeds and encouraged by the locally published *Northern Star*. In the same month the Northern Political Union was established at Newcastle. Chartism emerged as a confederation of a number of regionally based organisations such as these. Although this widened the agitation and gave it a truly national character, it also created organisational difficulties. The tendency to fragment was an ever-present problem throughout the movement's existence.

But in these early stages the mass potential of Chartism was clear. At a meeting in Birmingham, in August 1838, 200,000 people saw Attwood and O'Connor share the same platform. 250,000 turned out for a similar occasion at Peep Green, in the West Riding, in October. In assessing the significance of the large numbers at these meetings it is worth remembering that a Wembley Cup Final crowd today contains somewhere around 90,000 people.

In September 1838 John Fielden chaired one of these huge meetings just outside Manchester. One of the speakers, along with Oastler, Stephens and O'Connor, was Robert Lowery, a tailor by trade and a delegate from Newcastle. In his autobiography he described the day:

1 Local and district processions soon began to fill the streets and we joined them. Although I had often seen 100,000 at a meeting in Newcastle I never had a clear conception of a multitude until that day. The day was exceedingly fine, and there were processions from
5 Rochdale and Oldham and the chief places for fourteen miles or upwards around Manchester; I should think there were hundreds of bands of music. I could not conceive where the people came from, for at every open space or corner there would be thousands standing, besides the crowd passing. When we got out of the streets it was an
10 exciting sight to see the processions arriving on the Moor from different places, with their flags flying and the music of the bands swelling the air, ever and anon over-topped by a loud cheer which ran along the different lines. On ascending the hustings a still more exciting sight awaited us. *The Times* estimated the meeting at about 300,000. One
15 dense mass of faces beaming with earnestness – as far as you could distinguish faces – then beyond still an immense crowd, but with indistinct countenances. There is something in the appearance of such multitudes, – permeated with one thought or feeling, whom no building made with human hands could hold, met beneath the mighty dome of God's sub-
20 lime and beautiful creation, and appealing to Him for a cause which they believe to be right and just, – something which for the moment, seems to realise the truths of the ancient saying – 'The voice of the people is as the voice of God.'

The 53 delegates elected at these and many other meetings came together as the General Convention of the Industrious Classes in London in February 1839. The next few months were spent debating a range of issues including that of 'ulterior measures', or what would be done if the petition was rejected. High on the list of possibilities was the idea of a general strike or 'sacred month'. The petition itself was to be presented in June.

b) The Ideology and Organisation of Chartism

In many ways Chartism resembled the political reform movements that had preceded it. The language used referred back to Thomas

Paine's analysis in the *Rights of Man*. The Chartists saw themselves as representing 'the People', that is, all those excluded from political participation by 'Old Corruption'. They also saw themselves standing for the true 'Constitution' (though unlike the United States Britain never had a written Constitution). Like Paine, they saw the vote was one of a number of 'natural rights' which no government could legitimately withhold from the People. In this respect the six points of the Charter were essentially an eighteenth-century radical agenda. The historian Gareth Stedman Jones, in his book *Languages of Class* (1984), has argued that this was a weakness in the movement. Faced with the development of a new industrial society, the Chartists could only deploy the language of eighteenth-century radicalism through which to analyse their experience. This meant that they worked essentially with a political, rather than an economic analysis of their position; the enemy was 'Old Corruption' rather than the competitive market economy. When, in the 1840s and 1850s, successive governments began to introduce reforms (for example, the repeal of the Corn Laws in 1846 or the 1847 Ten Hours Act, restricting factory hours) it became more and more difficult to identify the government as 'Old Corruption' and support for Chartism fell away.

The Chartists also drew strength from the religious revival that had occurred alongside industrialisation in areas like South Wales, the Black Country, Lancashire and the West Riding. It is true that the movement included a Republican strand which, in its condemnation of both the Church and the Monarchy, began its meetings with the sentiment, 'May the last King be strangled with the entrails of the last Bishop'. But for the most part the Chartists rejected what they called 'priestianity', whilst endorsing Christianity. It was common for Chartist speakers to end their meetings with the Old Testament warcry, 'to your tents O Israel!'. A popular Chartist activity was to pack a Church on Sunday, arriving before the usual congregation. When the priest arrived he would be asked to preach from what was seen as a socially radical passage of the Bible. A firm Chartist favourite was James v, verses 1–6, beginning, 'Go to now, ye rich men, weep and howl ...'.

If Chartism broke little new ground in terms of the ideas behind the movement, its political strategy was also fairly familiar, based as it was on what historians call 'the platform'. Huge, peaceful, public meetings served notice on the government of the strength of feeling in the country and this, of course, drew heavily on the experience of the Reform Bill campaign. The 'language of menace' which Chartist speakers often employed, and which caused consternation among middle-class observers, simply recalled the platform orations of the 'Days of May'. Attwood led the way here, dusting off his old speeches and re-presenting his audiences with his well-worked notion of 'wholesome terror'. As he put it to the August 1838 meeting, 'No blood shall be shed by us; but if our enemies shed blood – if they attack the people – they must take the consequences upon their own heads.' The right to defend oneself if attacked, or 'defensive violence', had been invoked a good deal during the Reform Bill campaign. It was also a central feature of the Chartist's strategy as they prepared themselves to face an unsympathetic government. Recalling 'Peterloo', the Chartists expected that the government might well take direct action against even a peaceful movement. There was some disagreement among the Chartists themselves over just how 'ready' they should be; some advocating arming in preparation. But despite these differences there was a general agreement that if it became the subject of attack the movement had the right to defend itself, a right which Attwood had invoked to good effect in 1832. This commitment to defensive violence was often expressed in forthright terms, as with the slogan of the Newcastle Chartists, 'If they Peterloo us, we'll Moscow them!' (a reference to Napoleon's razing of the Russian capital in 1812). Yet for all this the movement was a predominantly peaceful one which aimed to utilise the constitutional right to petition Parliament for a redress of grievances. The Chartist slogan, 'Peacefully if we can, forcibly if we must', neatly summed up the order of strategic priorities.

Again, there was nothing new in the strategy of petitioning. But this was to be the 'last' petition: a statement of public opinion so overwhelming in size no government could ignore it. British radicals had also toyed with the idea of establishing a Convention since the early days of the French Revolution, and always with the idea that such a body should carry symbolic significance. Many contemporaries (and not a few historians since) considered it rather quaint that members of the Convention put the letters 'MC' after their names, in the way that a Member of Parliament might put 'MP'. But this was more than mere affectation. Convention members had been elected by a show of hands at nationwide public meetings. The Convention, it was therefore thought, represented the 'people' in a way that the Commons, elected on a restricted franchise, did not. The idea was that the Convention would meet in the Capital, as a shining alternative to a corrupt Parliament – a kind of 'anti-Parliament'. As O'Connor put it in August 1838 (whilst slightly under-estimating final delegate numbers):

1 When they had 49 delegates in London, let them attend them to the number of 300,000 or 400,000 with a petition on their shoulders to the door of the House of Commons and let them tell the House of Commons that the constituency of England were waiting in the Palace-
5 yard for an answer.

Yet, despite these similarities, Chartism differed from the agitations that had preceded it in two important respects. First, in the sheer scale and organisation of the movement, and second, in its increasingly clear development as an essentially working-class movement. Both these points can best be illustrated by a detailed analysis of Chartist support.

c) Who Were the Chartists? Working-Class Support and Middle-Class Withdrawal

Chartism attracted support from the new industrial districts throughout the country. Asa Briggs argued in his book *Chartist Studies* (1959) that Chartism recruited better in the older, decaying trades of the increasingly outmoded domestic system, rather than among the newer factory workers. However, this view has not been sustained by closer research. Chartism's support did not only come from the handloom weavers of Lancashire and Yorkshire or the framework knitters of the East Midlands. It also came from among the cotton spinners of Lancashire and Lanarkshire and the colliers of South Wales and the North-East. Chartism also drew upon the traditional trades common to all localities, like tailoring, the building crafts, and shoemaking.

Chartism was widely supported by women, even though the Chartists only demanded manhood suffrage and were ambivalent over the issue of political rights for women. Dorothy Thompson, in her book *The Chartists* (1984), has traced over 100 female radical associations formed to agitate for the Charter. Her analysis is extended in Jutta Schwarzkopf's study *Women in the Chartist Movement* (1991), where a history of active involvement by women is again evidenced. Nevertheless, it is clear that Chartism was a male-dominated (patriarchal) organisation. Its working-class male membership accepted the widely held view that men and women should occupy separate spheres; the public sphere was the preserve of the man, the domestic sphere that of the woman. So, women appeared in Chartism mainly in the roles of radical wives and mothers. They were marginalised within the national leadership, though they may have had more influence in local and informal organisations than has previously been appreciated. Local Yorkshire activist Ben Wilson remembered his aunt as a formative influence on his political education: 'she was a famous politician, a Chartist and a great admirer of Feargus O'Connor'.

The breadth of Chartist support meant that it could, therefore, lay claim to being a national movement in what was still an intensely regional society. The nature of its organisation recognised that its strength lay in the localities. Delegates were constantly returning to their regions to confer or to relay information and to generate discussion. The Convention allocated 'social missionaries' to particular regions to maintain support. Local self-help groups, co-operatives, and schools were created in many areas. Above all the Chartist press, particularly the *Northern Star,* reported events in the regions and this gave a sense of national participation. By July 1839 sales of the *Star* were as high as 60,000 a week.

The existence of a common programme and the movement's organisational framework, popularised by its national press, meant that Chartism was always more than a series of local responses to industrialisation. The issue of disunity has figured so strongly in accounts of Chartism's failure, over the years, that it is easy to overlook the degree of cohesion that was achieved. This was all the more remarkable given the opposition of the authorities, the physical distance between regions and the poverty of most Chartists. Nevertheless, aware of the fragility of their confederation, the Convention decided in May 1839 to move to Birmingham so as to be closer to its basis of support in the Midlands, the North, Scotland and South Wales.

In these early months Chartism also attracted participation from those members of the middle class who had been disappointed by the fruits of the Reform Act. As we have seen, the campaigns against excessive factory hours, and the application of the New Poor Law, drew together a working alliance from across the social spectrum united around two clearly defined moral issues: child labour and the relief of the poor. For working people the extension of these single issue campaigns into the broader demand for universal manhood suffrage seemed logical, given the failure of Parliament to respond to pressure. A government elected under the provisions of the Charter would, it was felt, repeal both the New Poor Law and the Corn Laws, abolish what remained of the 'taxes on knowledge', ensure the rights of trade unions, and introduce a Ten Hours Act. These issues were generally associated with a raising of living standards and an improvement in the quality of life, topics of enormous concern to working-class audiences in times of depression. Owenism had reminded working people of their economic importance to an industrial society and they looked to the Charter to realise their full and just rewards. In his biography of O'Connor, historian James Epstein refers to this as the 'implicit social programme' of Chartism.

However, for the middle classes the advocacy of universal suffrage was fraught with difficulties. It was all very well for the Chartists to argue that 'labour is the source of all wealth', but if a society was based on this assumption where would this leave the employers? To put this another way, to what extent was the demand for trade union rights, embodied in Chartist support for the transported Glasgow spinners, compatible with the desire of industrialists to run their businesses as they saw fit? If the vote were given to the propertyless, how would they act towards the propertied?

These central questions, relating to the way the working classes might exercise the vote, if they received it, were put to one side during the first few months of the movement. Francis Place estimated that, of the original Convention delegates, 24 were working men and 29 from other ranks in society. Yet, by May 1839, a large number of the middle-class delegates had resigned, most notably all seven elected from the Political Council of the BPU.

These resignations were triggered ostensibly by the Convention's advocacy of 'physical force'. In November 1838 the Revd J.R.

Stephens was arrested for the violence of a speech he gave at Hyde in Lancashire. In April 1839 riots broke out at Llanidloes in mid Wales, when the Metropolitan Police were drafted in to arrest local Chartists. In June, when Attwood presented the petition with its 1,280,000 signatures to the House of Commons, his support for it was clearly wavering. Although disappointed by the Reform Act of 1832, Attwood's support for universal suffrage had never been enthusiastic. His preference would have been for a more limited franchise linked to a property qualification (household suffrage). In fact, he renounced the movement shortly after and this was, to some extent, presaged in his remarks to the Commons:

1 Although he most cordially supported the petition, was ready to support every word contained in it, was determined to use every means in his power in order to carry it out into a law, he must say, that many reports had gone abroad, in regard to arguments said to have been used
5 in support of the petition on different occasions, which he distinctly disavowed. He never, in the whole course of his life, recommended any means, or inculcated any doctrine except peace, law, order, loyalty and union, and always in good faith, not holding one face out of doors, and another in the House; but always in the same manner, and in the same
10 feeling, fairly, and openly doing all that he could as a man, a patriot, and a Christian, to work out the principles which he maintained; and to support the views of the petitioners. He washed his hands of any idea, of any appeal to physical force.

O'Connor's response was direct. 'Had none of the Birmingham leaders ever used strong words?', he asked in the *Star*. Given Attwood's position in the 'Days of May', and his pronouncements in 1838, the elevation of violent rhetoric into a significant issue in 1839 is worth a closer look. Of course, it raised the crucial question of whether the working class were simply a mob or a group able to exercise the responsibilities of citizenship. So there is a debate within a debate here. What is really being discussed is the issue of working-class responsibility. Looking back on his experience of Chartism, a disillusioned Attwood wrote: 'There is no instance in history in which political movements have been successful without leaders and in almost every instance those leaders have been men of wealth and influence.' Working-class delegates to the Convention did not see it like this. Nor did they intend necessarily to accept middle-class leadership after the Charter had been accepted. As one working-class Chartist put it, referring to the role of the middle class: 'Did they think they were going to lead the working men by the nose any longer?' The gradual realisation that the working-class delegates at the Convention were looking forward to the exercise of power made many middle-class participants uncomfortable. Put simply, from a middle-class perspective, it was one thing to agree with working people over specific issues like the Poor Law or child labour, or to sympathise in general terms with the 'poor', but it was another thing entirely to have them run the country.

The supporters with real doubts about universal suffrage, like Oastler, Stephens and Attwood, soon left the movement. Those men of the middle ranks who remained in Chartism accepted that it emerged from an articulate and self-confident working class. They were often from the lower middle class, a group that had been so important in the French Revolution. In this category one might include disaffected professionals, like the Scottish doctor Peter Murray McDouall, elected to the convention to represent Ashton-under-Lyne, or the lawyer Bronterre O'Brien elected for Manchester. Others were shopkeepers, such as linen draper John Frost of Newport or beer-house keeper Peter Bussey of Bradford. A few, like O'Connor, were in the 'gentleman reformer' mould of Burdett and Hunt. These men remained in Chartism, alongside working-class leaders like the tailor Robert Lowery or the cabinet-maker William Lovett, because they accepted the implications of a political programme based on universal suffrage.

d) Rejection and Reaction. The Bull Ring Riots and the Newport Uprising

The resignations of middle-class members of the Convention, in the Spring of 1839, points to the growth of tension and apprehension around the submission of the petition. The expectation of a hostile government response increased the talk of armed resistance. On 4 July 1839 rioting broke out in the Bull Ring in Birmingham when the Mayor used a detachment of the Metropolitan Police to break up a Chartist meeting. This was particularly unfortunate since the Mayor had been an early supporter of Chartism, though his enthusiasm had diminished upon his election to office. Other middle-class ex-delegates to the Convention were now local councillors and magistrates and were thus involved in the decision to use the police. Also, as local Chartists pointed out, the town's middle class had encouraged such meetings in the Bull Ring (a market place) during the Reform Bill campaign. The Convention, now sitting in Birmingham, condemned the attack in a placard composed by William Lovett, who was the Convention's secretary, and published by its Chairman John Collins, a local tool fitter. The rioting that followed the introduction of the hated London police lasted sporadically for a fortnight. It was exacerbated by the news that the petition had been rejected by 235 votes to 46. Not only had the Charter been rejected but a majority of MPs had not even bothered to attend the vote.

An extract from Lovett's placard gives some insights to the riots in the Bull Ring and perhaps casts light on the movement as a whole. A court would later judge it to be a seditious libel.

1   That this Convention is of opinion that a wanton, flagrant, and unjust
    outrage has been made upon the people of Birmingham by a blood-
    thirsty and unconstitutional force from London, acting under the auth-
    ority of men who, when out of office, sanctioned and took part in the
5   meetings of the people; and now, when they share in public plunder,
    seek to keep the people in social slavery and political degradation.

Lovett and Collins spent a year in prison for writing and publishing
this document. Historians have traditionally been eager to divide the
Chartist leadership into those who supported 'physical force' and
those who rejected violence and advocated 'moral force' alone.
Lovett is generally seen as the prime example of a 'moral force'
Chartist. It is worth noting, therefore, that even Lovett, with his
acknowledged predilection against the use of arms, was prepared to
go to prison to support the 'right' of violent self-defence. In his view
the attack was unconstitutional and the people of Birmingham had
every right to defend themselves.

The issue of defensive violence was something about which there
could be broad agreement within the movement. But the Newport
Uprising of November 1839 was clearly violence of a different order
altogether. Following the petition's rejection, the Convention dissolved itself in some disarray in September. Preparations for a rising
went ahead in secret in South Wales. On 2 November, with an inac-
curacy it must later have regretted, one local paper declared Chartism
to be 'extinct' in the Newport area. The next night nearly 10,000
men, mostly colliers and iron workers from the valleys, armed with
pikes and firearms, marched in close military formation on the town.
Led by local Chartist leaders John Frost, Zepania Williams and
William Jones, the advance column clashed with troops firing from
the Westgate Hotel in the town square. After a skirmish the Chartists
fled leaving between 20 and 30 of their number dead.

At their trial Frost, Williams and Jones were capitally convicted of
high treason. The prosecution alleged that Newport was planned as
the first blow in a nationwide, co-ordinated, uprising. Defending a
plea of not guilty, the three men claimed that their actions had been
intended as a sort of monster demonstration of strength to protest
against the recent arrest of the local Convention 'missionary' Henry
Vincent. Neither of these contemporary explanations is entirely convincing. On the one hand, it seems unlikely that Newport was part of
a concerted plan for insurrection. Offensive violence of this sort was
rejected as simply too dangerous by most Chartist leaders. O'Connor
consistently argued that a citizen army would be massacred by regular
troops, a point which the events at Newport seem to have borne out.
On the other hand, many of the participants do not seem to have seen
the affair as simply a demonstration that went horribly wrong.
Between 500 and 600 of the Chartists had guns and all marched in
companies or brigades led by 'captains'. One Chartist, a 17-year-old
cabinet-maker named George Shell, wrote to his parents before set-

ting off: 'I shall this night be engaged in a struggle for freedom and should it please God to spare my life I shall see you soon; but if not, grieve not for me, I shall fall in a noble cause.' Shell died in the first exchange of gunfire.

It seems likely that Chartists in the tight-knit communities of the Welsh valleys aimed at a swift seizure of Newport to serve as an inspiration to Chartists in other areas. Two points, at least, do seem clear. First, that armed insurrection, of the sort seen at Newport, was not a typical element of Chartist strategy. Where violence occurred in connection with Chartism it was generally in the form of riots where the crowd and the authorities confronted each other in the traditional fashion of the food riot. The armed overthrow of the state by force of arms interested only a tiny minority of Chartists. Second, the death sentences on Frost, Williams and Jones (commuted to transportation for life), encouraged the authorities throughout the country to round up the Chartist leadership in their areas. Nearly 500 people served prison terms between 1839 and 1841 for offences related to Chartist activity.

e) Re-organisation and the Second Petition

The failure of the first petition, and the mass arrests during the winter that followed, painfully demonstrated to the Chartists the powerful opposition they faced. The Reform Act had given the existing parliamentary system renewed strength and confidence. This was the lesson of the first phase of Chartism and it led to prolonged wrangling within the movement over strategy and the way forward. Given the locally based nature of Chartism, and its tendency to fragment, there was clearly a need for a strong, centralised organisation. Encouraged by O'Connor, in *Northern Star* articles written from his cell in York Castle, the National Charter Association (NCA) was established in Manchester in July 1840. This was to exist for a decade as the most important of the Chartist organisations. By the summer of 1842 it boasted 400 branches throughout the country and a membership of 50,000. The NCA organised the collection of 3 million signatures for a second Chartist petition, presented to Parliament by a new Convention in July 1842. This was the period of Chartism's greatest strength, yet the petition was rejected by a Commons vote of 287 to 46.

The NCA was not the only Chartist organisation in the 1840s and it is the debates and disputes between the leaders of the various factions that has led to the argument that Chartism failed as a result of internal disunity. Whilst in prison, Lovett and Collins drew up a plan for a national system of education for the working community. This scheme, complete with schools, libraries and teacher training colleges, would be financed by a weekly penny contribution from the signatories of the first Chartist petition. Lovett and Collins argued that a formally educated working class would not be denied the vote. In a similar way Henry Vincent and Robert Lowery (whose account of an open-air meeting was examined earlier) began the Chartist Teetotal Association. They were convinced that if working people publicly rejected alcohol they would prove their fitness for the franchise. Arthur O'Neill, a Nonconformist minister from Glasgow, established a Chartist Church in Birmingham in 1841, arguing that the vote might be earned by adopting avowedly Christian behaviour. These 'new moves', as they were called, aimed to achieve the vote by explicitly 'moral force' strategies. A public demonstration of moral rectitude by the working class would disarm the major argument against its enfranchisement.

None of these initiatives ever gained the level of support achieved by the NCA, under O'Connor's leadership. This did not mean that the NCA, or O'Connor, rejected education, sobriety, or Christian behaviour. They simply felt that the Charter must come first. O'Connor argued that if the vote really was a right, then it was absurd to talk of people having to 'qualify' for it. Nobody would argue, for example, that one should have to sign the pledge before being entitled to enjoy, say, equality before the law or freedom of conscience. The NCA felt the same point applied to the 'moral force' schemes for achieving the vote. The debate between these groups was often acrimonious. But it is important to note that the NCA position, though different from that held by the 'new movers', was itself a 'moral force' position. The major difference was that the NCA retained its primary commitment to the orthodox strategy of petitioning.

Similar debates took place around the overtures being made to the Chartists at this time by some middle-class radicals. In 1839 a group of middle-class men, led by two textile manufacturers Richard Cobden and John Bright, established the Anti-Corn Law League in Manchester. Cobden felt that the continued dominance of the aristocracy after 1832 was symbolised by the laws preventing a free trade in corn. The League argued that, given the importance of bread in the diet of the workforce, a free trade in corn would allow all aspects of the economy to flourish. They were encouraged in this view by the impact of the depression of 1838–42. The League established Operative Corn Law Associations which manufacturers tried to persuade their workers to join. But, whilst the League's objective of repeal was achieved in 1846, the Operative Associations never attracted large numbers of people. The Chartists saw the League as a distraction from the main business of achieving the Charter. A Parliament elected on the basis of universal suffrage would soon repeal the hated Corn Laws.

Yet the League needed the numerical support of the working community, just as this had been required to achieve middle-class ends in 1832. In the words of Cobden the workers would be 'something in our rear to frighten the aristocracy'. With this in mind the free traders made two attempts to wrest the political leadership of the working class from the Chartists by trying to re-establish the alliance that had been so effective in 1832. The Leeds Reform Association, established by leading members of the Anti-Corn Law League in 1841, invited the Chartists to support a programme of household suffrage. Its founding meeting was boycotted by the NCA. O'Connor dubbed it the 'Fox and Goose Club', (a club for working-class 'geese' run by middle-class 'foxes'). Those Chartists, like John Collins, who did attend, did so simply to persuade the Association to switch to universal suffrage. They left when they failed in this attempt. Collins, who was more willing than most Chartists to negotiate with the middle classes, took great encouragement from the failure of the Leeds Reform Association since, in his view it 'proved that the day was gone by when any middle-class man could dictate what was to be done.'

A second initiative was pushed from within the League by the Quaker corn merchant Joseph Sturge. His Complete Suffrage Union (CSU) accepted the 'People's Charter', with all six points, in everything but name. Sturge argued that the name carried violent connotations and therefore it was not acceptable. The Chartists were exceptionally suspicious of this position. After all, they had recent experience of Attwood's half-hearted conversion to universal suffrage, and, in the atmosphere of mistrust that prevailed, Sturge's plan appeared to be a move of a similar order. Without the Chartist support it strove for, the CSU was effectively dead by the end of 1842. The failure of these initiatives suggests that the lessons of 1832 had been learned by the Chartists. For them, an alliance with the middle class had to involve acceptance of both universal suffrage and working-class participation in the leadership. The Anti-Corn Law League, for example, was happy to have a Chartist rank and file but did not want working men on their executive councils. John Bright considered the vote a 'trust' rather than a 'right'.

The bitterness of the relationship between the classes manifested itself in a series of strikes in the Midlands and North in the summer of 1842. These were sparked by reductions in wages and the rejection of the second petition. In August, workers in the textile towns of Lancashire and Yorkshire went from factory to factory calling on their fellows to join the strike and removing the plugs from the steam engine boilers so that work would cease. The 'Plug strikes' spread south to the Potteries of Staffordshire and the metal-working towns of the Black Country, both strong Chartist areas. Troops were used to suppress the strikes and this led to extensive rioting and another round-up of both the local and the national Chartist leadership. If anything, Peel's Tory government, elected in 1841, were even firmer in their dealings with the Chartists than the Whigs had been. It has been estimated that around 1,500 people were brought before the courts for related offences by the end of the year.

f) The Land Plan and the Third Chartist Petition

From the high point of its popularity in 1842, Chartism entered into a decline. The failure of two petitions, and the government repression that followed, shook the belief in political solutions. An improvement in trade from 1843 led working people to turn to trade unions. Demands for higher wages were always more likely to be successful when labour was needed. Practical, small-scale schemes with immediate and obvious benefits began to replace the elusive and visionary objectives of Chartism. In 1844, for example, a group of ex-Chartists formed the Rochdale Co-operative Society. This revived the old idea of retail shops which distributed their profits between their customers. The initiative of the 'Rochdale Pioneers' encouraged similar co-operative societies in other localities and these quickly became a familiar feature of working-class self-help. By 1844 the *Northern Star* was failing to reach its break even point of 4,000 sales per week. O'Connor, however, arrested this decline by launching his Land Plan, a pet scheme he had been contemplating for years.

The Chartist Land Company, established in 1845, aimed to establish rural communities in which working families would own their own small patch of land. Chartists were invited to buy shares in the Company and thus qualify for location in such a community. The scheme was phenomenally successful in attracting subscribers. By 1848 around 100,000 people throughout the country were members of local branches of the Land Company. Five communities were opened by 1848, each with its own impressive facilities of schools, parks and baths. Yet the scheme was not a success. O'Connor was undoubtedly a charismatic speaker and an energetic leader; he set about promoting the Land Plan with characteristic single-minded fervour. But he was not a good administrator. Although he was an inveterate optimist, even he was unprepared for the degree of support engendered by the scheme and the Company's accounts were constantly in a state of chaos. Besides this, the government was openly hostile. In 1848 it set up a Select Committee to investigate the Company's affairs, hoping to uncover enough corruption to destroy O'Connor's reputation. Actually, the Committee found that not only had O'Connor acted with probity, but also that the Land Company owed him £3,000. Yet the Company was declared illegal and wound up. Places in the communities were being allocated on the basis of a ballot and this element of chance meant that the Company could not be deemed a Friendly Society as it had claimed. Without the protection of the Friendly Societies' legislation the Company was actually an illegal body. There seems little doubt that worry over the welfare of the Land Company contributed to O'Connor's sudden descent into insanity in 1851 and his death four years later.

It had never been O'Connor's intention to re-locate all workers on the land. He simply aimed to provide an acceptable alternative to industrial work that would reduce unemployment and thus keep up the wages of all workers. The plan's popularity suggests that O'Connor had tapped a significant nerve among the world's first industrial workforce, many of whom clearly hungered for a return to the land. Yet industrial workers made poor farmers and none of the communities thrived. In O'Connor's mind the communities would be centres for radical political thought and Chartist culture. But this was disputed by other leaders. Bronterre O'Brien and the Leicester Chartist, Thomas Cooper, agreed with other influential observers, such as Marx and Engels, that the communities might create a 'peasant class' of small proprietors. If the experience of European countries was anything to go by, such a group was likely, by virtue of its ownership of property, to be reactionary rather than radical in politics. However, the scale of the plan's support reminds us how close this new urban society was to its rural roots, at least in the mind of its workforce.

The European revolutions of 1848 put political solutions back on the agenda. At home an economic depression created the backdrop to Chartism's last initiative as a mass movement. A number of Chartist candidates had stood in the general election of 1847, at which a Whig government had been returned to office under Lord John Russell. In an electrifying campaign, O'Connor had been elected for Nottingham. Inspired by this and by the revolution in Paris in February 1848, a Chartist convention met in London in April 1848 to organise the delivery of a third petition to Parliament. This was to follow a mass meeting on 10 April at Kennington Common (roughly the spot where the Oval cricket ground stands today).

Perhaps the most remarkable feature of the events surrounding the submission of the third petition is the response it engendered in the military authorities. Besides the 7,122 regular troops, 1,231 pensioners and 4,000 policemen available in London in April 1848, Russell's government also authorised the enrolment of 85,000 special constables, mostly men from the middle class. The meeting planned for 10 April was declared illegal. The Queen was evacuated to Osborne House on the Isle of Wight, although some feared that even this would not be sufficient to protect the sovereign. As the Foreign Secretary, Lord Palmerston, put it to the Prime Minister, 'the Solent Sea is not impassable'.

Defying the ban, the Chartists, under the leadership of O'Connor and Ernest Jones, went ahead with their meeting. An early photograph of this survives and shows working men in their Sunday best, listening to speakers addressing the crowd from a cart draped with the words 'Labour is the source of all wealth'. An orderly procession can be seen leaving the field in the background. However, the procession was stopped before it reached Westminster. After a calming speech from O'Connor, the meeting of about 20,000 dispersed peacefully. O'Connor and a small group proceeded in a cab, with the petition, to the House of Commons. A parliamentary committee swiftly declared that, of the five and a half million signatures on the petition, less than two million were genuine. In the light of this the Commons decided not to receive the petition formally.

A myth has grown up that Chartism died of shame on 10 April 1848. This was how many contemporaries chose to see the events. Some historians, on the other hand, argue that this was O'Connor's finest hour. Actually, the Chartists themselves were inclined to see the day as a 'triumph', in that it passed off without bloodshed despite the government's apparent determination to provoke a final confrontation with the movement. Much of the credit for this must go to O'Connor. Unfortunately, his restraint on the day has been widely seen as cowardice. Also, Chartism, though never as strong in 1848 as in 1839 or 1842, actually continued to grow after 10 April. Palmerston, at least, recognised this, arguing 'the snake is scotched not killed'. In May 1848 a Chartist National Assembly gathered in London and in the same month 60,000 people met on Clerkenwell Green. The summer of 1848 saw a series of disturbances centred on Bradford, Manchester and Liverpool as local authorities broke up Chartist gatherings. All this activity was met by the arrest and trial of nearly 300 Chartists. By the winter of 1848 the movement was down for the third time and, effectively, out. Although it would struggle on for another ten years, it would never again be a mass movement.

The Kennington Common meeting, 10 April 1848, a contemporary print of the mass meeting that preceeded the submission of the third petition.

3 The Failure of Chartism: Contemporary and Historical Explanations

> **KEY ISSUE** Was Chartism simply a product of economic hardship or should we consider it to be a serious political movement?

Chartism has had many historians and invariably they have addressed the issue of why the movement failed. The various explanations offered over the years reflect the many different constructions that it is possible to put upon the nature of Chartism. Undoubtedly the most compact and convenient explanation of the movement's rise and fall is that which sees it as a kind of 'hunger politics' on a large scale. The three periods of Chartist strength, 1839, 1842 and 1848, were also periods of intense distress whereas the movement disappeared forever in the improved economic conditions of the mid-Victorian period. This was certainly the perception of the many middle-class contemporary observers who expressed themselves concerned with what was called the 'Condition of England Question' in the 1830s and the 1840s. These people saw the grim conditions in the large towns as an offence to a Christian nation and also as a tangible threat to order and morality. The political philosopher Thomas Carlyle, writing in 1839, described Chartism as 'bitter discontent grown fierce and mad'. Although he sympathised with the workforce who, he could see, lived in appalling conditions, he also feared what he saw as their latent irrationality. Another sympathetic contemporary observer was the novelist Elizabeth Gaskell. The wife of a Unitarian minister in Manchester, she had first-hand knowledge of working-class living conditions through her charity work. When she came to examine Chartism, in her novel *Mary Barton,* she stressed the relationship between hunger and the framing of the first petition:

1 Besides, the starving multitudes had heard that the very existence of
   their distress had been denied in Parliament; and though they felt this
   strange and inexplicable, yet the idea that their misery had still to be
   revealed in all its depths, and that then some remedy would be found,
5 soothed their aching hearts and kept down their rising fury.
       So a petition was framed, and signed by thousands in the bright
   Spring days of 1839, imploring Parliament to hear witnesses who could
   testify to the unparalleled destitution of the manufacturing districts.

In fact, Gaskell omits to mention in her novel that Chartism had any political objectives. Her reference, in the above extract to the 'starving multitudes', is also uncomfortably close to Edmund Burke's reference to a 'swinish multitude'.

In much the same way the Revd J.R. Stephens announced to a meeting in 1838 that Chartism was really a 'knife and fork question'.

Yet any analysis which over-simplifies the relationship between hunger and Chartism will inevitably see the movement's rank and file as an unthinking group responding only to very basic stimuli. Charting the incidence of trade slumps may help to clarify the chronology of Chartism, but this is only a starting point. The historian really needs to explain why this particular group of hungry people campaigned for the vote. Chartism grew from a political awareness, but Gaskell, as an outsider looking into the working community, may not have been aware of this dimension. Possibly the Revd J.R. Stephen's personal reservations about the need for universal suffrage also led him to play down this aspect. His 'knife and fork' statement may have been wishful thinking; this is what he would have preferred Chartism to have been about. His early departure from the movement suggests that some disparity existed between the way he saw the Chartists and the way they saw themselves.

Certainly the fear of a hungry, uneducated, and therefore unpredictable, mob lay at the heart of contemporary fears of conceding the vote to the working class. In the debate on the second petition, in the House of Commons in 1842, the flavour of this view came through strongly in the words of the Whig MP for Edinburgh, T.B. Macauley:

> I believe that universal suffrage would be fatal for all purposes for which government exists, and for which aristocracies exist, and that it is utterly incompatible with the very existence of civilisation.

His remarks, of course, recall again those of Burke on the 'swinish multitude' half a century before. Yet the closer we get to the Chartists themselves the more this seems to be an inaccurate picture based on fear or a lack of knowledge. There is certainly some distance between Macauley's attack on universal suffrage and the defence of the measure published the year before in the Scottish newspaper the *Chartist Circular:*

> ... it is the only security against bad laws, and for good government, which otherwise depend on the caprice or fears of the master-class, who make laws; and while the exclusive few have a profitable interest in bad laws there will be no barrier to tyranny and corruption ...

Economic depression was clearly a mainspring for increasing Chartist support and activity but it acted upon a community with its own political traditions and beliefs. In this sense hunger was a great educator. An industrial society that could not deliver full employment, or feed its workforce adequately, advertised itself as ripe for reform. Those thrown out of work found themselves confronted with the awful reality of the New Poor Law. The experience of distress was a major stimulant to Chartism because it led thousands to ask political questions about how poverty came about. Economic crisis also closed down the alternative forms of self-help available to the working community. Trade unions could not flourish in periods of depression

because workers had nothing with which to bargain. Thus it is possible to identify an oscillation in working-class organisation between
political protest in bad times and union activity in good times. If this
is so, Chartism represents a pragmatic and reasoned response to
changing circumstances rather than being, as contemporaries feared,
an irrational response to hunger.

Yet many historians have shared at least some of the contemporary
view and have argued that Chartism failed because of the political and
intellectual immaturity of the working people who made up its ranks.
The working class were not yet 'ready' for the vote. This, it is often
felt, was reflected in the internal disunity of the movement and in the
failure of the main body of Chartists to distinguish between reliable
leaders and charlatans. This approach is particularly clear in the historical treatment of Feargus O'Connor. The first history of Chartism
was written in 1854 by R.G. Gammage, an ex-Chartist. Gammage had
fallen out with O'Connor and in his *History of the Chartist Movement* he
laid the blame for the movement's failure squarely on O'Connor's
shoulders. O'Connor fared little better at the hands of later historians. Mark Hovell in his book *The Chartist Movement,* written in 1916
but still widely read today, lamented the fact that working people generally chose to follow O'Connor rather than the 'moral force' policies
of Lovett. Referring to the Chartists' 'dog-like' attachment to
O'Connor he dismisses him as a 'blustering, egotistical, blarneying,
managing, but intellectually and morally very unreliable Irishman,
who probably had never done an honest day's work in his life.'! This
remark tells us little about O'Connor but a good deal about Mark
Hovell. In fact, O'Connor was not an advocate of 'physical force'.
Rather, he put his faith in the constitutional strategy of the petition as
an expression of the public will.

The idealisation of Lovett by early historians of Chartism seems
misplaced. Lovett was influential in the early stages of the movement,
when, as we have seen, his contribution was profound. He drafted the
People's Charter, was Secretary to the Convention, and went to prison
for condemning the action of the Metropolitan Police in 1839. But his
plan for a Chartist education system to precede the achievement of
the Charter was never popular. Most Chartists adhered to the notion
that they had a right to the vote and that once this was secured other
reforms would follow. From 1842, when he joined with O'Connor to
defeat the CSU, his influence began to waver, as the popularity of the
National Charter Association grew. He was resurrected by historians
like Hovell because they were connected with the early twentieth-century Labour Party and Lovett seemed to fit the image of the ideal
Labour politician at this time. O'Connor, on the other hand, held the
movement together from 1841 onwards and built a national context
for its operations around his newspaper, The *Northern Star.* However,
as a platform orator and gentleman radical he fitted less well into the
way the twentieth-century Labour Party wished to view its antecedents.

But a view of the leadership is inseparable from an interpretation of the nature of the membership. For Hovell, and many others since, the Chartist membership demonstrated that it was not yet 'ready' to exercise the vote by following a 'mob-orator' like O'Connor. As a result their movement was fragmented and became hitched to an empty 'physical force' rhetoric with no political substance. This alienated friends in the middle class and antagonised the government, as a result of which the Charter was lost.

But Chartism was not made up of cowed and hungry simpletons. For its rank and file, as well as its leadership, radical politics represented a perfectly logical way of viewing their world and rectifying its abuses. The commitment to the vote stemmed from the brain rather than the belly. James Epstein's biography of O'Connor, *The Lion of Freedom* (1982) argues this point:

1   The consistent failure of historians to deal with O'Connor as a serious political leader, the assertion that he lacked principles and was willing to place his individual designs above the interests of the movement are not merely unfair to O'Connor but an implicit judgement upon the
5   thousands of working people who supported him.

Much of the interpretation of the movement seems to hang on the assumption that working people were uneducated. Whilst it is true that there was no formal system of schooling this does not mean that these were ignorant people.

If, on the other hand, we concentrate our attention on the opposition that Chartism faced it could be argued that the movement failed, not through inept leadership or internal disunity, but rather because successive governments refused to meet the demands of the Charter. The Chartists are often compared unfavourably with the Anti-Corn Law League whose objective was achieved in 1846. Yet these were two very different pressure groups and they met very different responses from government. One movement called for the removal of a single, though significant, piece of legislation. The other sought a fundamental change in the fabric of politics. The League's supporters were also voters and Peel's conversion to free-trade in the 1840s was sparked by a recognition that, if the aristocracy were to retain the reins of power, they would have to make concessions to the industrial middle class. It also had much to do with concern over the food supply following the Irish famine. But the Whig and Tory governments who refused the Chartist petitions in 1839, 1842 and 1848, clearly feared the consequences of granting the Charter far more than the dangers involved in turning it down. After the Reform Act the political system was relatively stable: the army remained loyal; the police force was extended to the large towns after the Municipal Corporations Act of 1835; and the new railway system meant that a swifter response from the forces of law and order was possible. In short, Chartism, a predominantly constitutional movement anyway, could be contained, and this was more acceptable than the massive political changes which an acceptance of the Charter would have involved.

Approaching Chartism in this way, historians writing in the left-wing tradition of E.P. Thompson (see page 16) have turned the orthodox interpretation on its head. They do not see Chartism as the product of hunger, with the labouring masses expressing their political immaturity by following irresponsible leaders. Instead, the movement is seen as the expression of political conviction from within communities that had often been involved in the fight for the vote since 1815. The common purpose and national organisation of the movement tends to be stressed in such interpretations. Dorothy Thompson, for example, argues that Chartism was 'the response of a literate and sophisticated working class'. She argues that Chartism was a class-conscious movement which represented a distinctive working-class perspective on society and politics. By this analysis, Chartism was an expression of the political maturity displayed by the working community. The failure of Chartism should not be seen to confirm that working people were somehow not yet 'ready' for the vote. Rather, the reverse was true: working people were eager and 'ready' to exercise political power but were prevented by a state made stable and confident by the Reform Act of 1832. From this point of view Chartism failed because it represented a political challenge to the established order of things. The acceptance of the petition would have created a very different sort of society and this was not something those who held power were prepared to contemplate. Instead, the governments of the day began to introduce reforms and this encouraged a belief in gradual change, rather than a sharp re-direction of the political system, as the six points implied.

The intensive scrutiny to which recent historians have subjected the movement has certainly served to emphasise the extent to which the Chartist experience shaped the lives of ordinary men and women. In the past, a concentration on the squabbles of the leadership has tended to obscure this point. Inspired by the work of Thomas Paine and the examples of men like Hunt and Cobbett, and an eighteenth-century tradition of radicalism, ordinary working people were prepared to confront the government of the world's most powerful nation armed, in most cases, with little more than rational argument.

Imprisonment involved horrific privations, yet respectable men and women were willing to undergo this ordeal for the sake of a political principle. Placed in this position in 1843 Lancashire Chartist Bernard McCartney told the court 'you may imprison my body but my mind will soar free'. This point was picked up in an editorial in the middle-class *Bradford Observer* newspaper in 1848. Commenting on recent Chartist arrests it observed that: 'they may be put down by physical force but they can be kept down only by moral force'. Chartism may have failed but its existence made an important statement about the presence of the working class in the new industrial society. Only the successful integration of this class into the political and authority systems of mid-Victorian society could ensure the social stability necessary for full economic expansion. The next chapter considers how this process of integration unfolded over the 35 years that followed the last Chartist petition.

Summary Diagram
Chartism

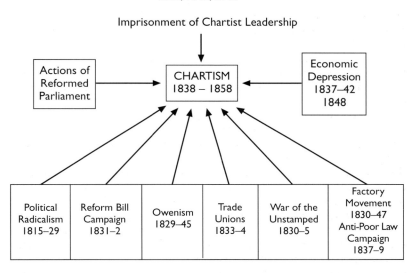

GOVERNMENT REJECTS
National Petition
1839, 1842, 1848

Imprisonment of Chartist Leadership

Actions of Reformed Parliament		CHARTISM 1838 – 1858		Economic Depression 1837–42 1848

| Political Radicalism 1815–29 | Reform Bill Campaign 1831–2 | Owenism 1829–45 | Trade Unions 1833–4 | War of the Unstamped 1830–5 | Factory Movement 1830–47 Anti-Poor Law Campaign 1837–9 |

Working on Chapter 3

Remember, any judgement on the rise or the demise of Chartism requires of you a consideration of the nature of the working community: What were its interests? What was it capable of? What influences was it subject to? Was it the 'swinish multitude' that Burke feared, or the 'starving multitude' that Gaskell depicts in her novel? Or was it the 'literate and sophisticated working class' that the historian Dorothy Thompson refers to in her study of the movement? Once your own opinion about the working community at the time is clear in your mind, you need to match this with the particular events of Chartist history.

One way of helping you to organise your material is to list points, drawn from this chapter, under the following two headings:

Chartism was a political movement.

Chartism was a national movement.

This exercise will provide you with the detail required for a better informed judgement on Chartist organisation and leadership.

Answering structured and essay questions on Chapter 3

An example of a structured question on Chartism might be as follows:

a) Why did Chartism emerge in 1838? *(5 marks)*
b) To what extent were government fears of Chartist violence justified? *(5 marks)*
c) How far are we right to see Chartism as simply 'hunger politics'? *(10 marks)*

Part a) asks you to focus on the factors surrounding the emergence of Chartism (and here you need to explore the contribution of radical movements leading up to 1838 and those short-term factors that relate more specifically to 1838 itself). In part b) you are asked to explore the potential for Chartist violence (look back over the chapter for sections on the Bull Ring riots, Newport, the 'language of menace' and the 1848 Kennington Common meeting). In part c) your view of the movement as a whole is required. Here you are making a judgement on the awareness and organisational capabilities of those involved in the movement. Beware particularly of the apparently easy answer. The hypothesis that Chartism rose with economic decline and failed when the economy recovered will appear to relieve you of the burden of a detailed knowledge of the movement. It does not; you will still need to explain, for example, why a 'hungry' working class read 60,000 copies of the *Northern Star* each week in 1839, why so many chose to express their hunger through politics, and so on. Hunger may provide the chronology of the movement but it does not explain why it took the form that it did.

Before embarking on essay questions on Chartism you should ask a question yourself: why do examiners love posing questions about Chartism? Movements that fail rarely draw such fulsome attention, and herein lies the paradox that makes all questions on Chartism so open to differing interpretation (and thus irresistible to examiners). Chartism was a *mass* movement, with *huge* support, which failed to achieve *any* of its objectives. Virtually all the questions you are likely to be asked on Chartism will require you to explore the relationship between mass support and abject failure.

Here are some typical examples of the sort of question that you might be asked involving your detailed knowledge of Chartism:

1. 'Its failure stemmed from inept leadership'. Discuss this verdict on the Chartist movement.
2. 'Chartism was a good deal more than a movement for social reform'. Discuss.
3. How much working-class solidarity was shown between 1838 and 1848?
4. To what extent did support for Chartism reflect the fluctuations in the British economy in the 1830s and 1840s?
5. With what justification have historians identified the growth of working-class consciousness between 1815 and 1850?
6. Did Chartism fail because lower-class unrest was basically a 'knife and fork' question?
7. How typical was Chartism of the popular radical movements in the first half of the nineteenth century?
8. Was Chartism primarily an economic or a political movement?

The focus of these questions varies, some of them place the nature of the movement in the foreground, some of them concentrate on the movement's failure, and others ask you to use Chartism as an exemplar of developments across a wider time-span. Yet all of them deal in some way with the *motivation* behind Chartism. Some are more explicit than others on the point that any consideration of the movement will involve you in the contentious issue of how far Chartism embodied a cohesive working-class political consciousness. To answer any of these questions you need not only to be able to give a considered overview of the movement, but also to support this by reference to the specific events and personalities involved.

Source-based questions on Chapter 3

1. Owenism

i) Examine the Labour note on page 41, and answer the following questions:

   a) Why were the Owenites so keen to base a currency on the hours of labour rather than on normal money? (*5 marks*)
   b) Some historians argue that such a scheme was 'bound' to fail. How far do you agree with their verdict? (*6 marks*)
   c) What can be learnt about the values and attitudes of the scheme's organisers from the design of the labour note? (*4 marks*)

2. The nature of Chartism

i) Read Robert Lowery's account of a Chartist meeting on page 50 and answer the following questions:

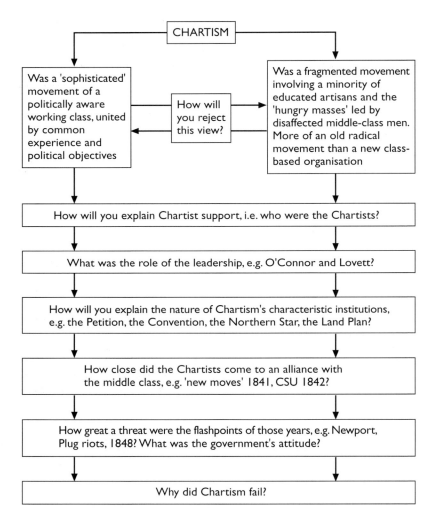

Chartism flow diagram. Bearing question 5 in mind, explore the possibilities of the flow diagram above. You are presented with two common, but very different, overviews of Chartism, both of which were dealt with in the chapter. Follow each through and try to see how you might interpret the detail of the movement if you held that view. Of course these are not the only models of explanation. You may, for example, wish to stress the highly regionalised nature of the movement (Chartism as a series of local responses). But whatever your view you need to match detail to interpretation and the diagram will help you to do this.

    a)   What is the significance of Lowery's decision to quote *The Times'* estimate of the numbers attending the meeting? (*2 marks*)
    b)   What impressed Lowery about the meeting? (*6 marks*)
    c)   Why did the Chartists hold meetings like this? (*7 marks*)

ii) Compare O'Connor's statement on petitioning and the Convention on page 52 with Lovett's placard issued after the Bull Ring riots, on page 57.
    a)   What is O'Connor suggesting the Chartists do? (*4 marks*)
    b)   Why does Lovett refer to the Metropolitan Police as an 'unconstitutional force'? (*4 marks*)
    c)   Historians often refer to 'physical force' or 'moral force' strategies. How well can these labels be applied to each of these statements? (*6 marks*)
    d)   Using your knowledge gained from a reading of this chapter, explain why the failure of Chartism is sometimes seen as a result of a divided leadership, and particularly in terms of the split between Lovett and O'Connor. (*8 marks*)

iii) Compare Macaulay and the *Chartist Circular* on the issue of universal suffrage (pages 64 and 65).
    a)   What are the 'purposes for which governments exist' that Macaulay refers to? (*2 marks*)
    b)   What does the *Chartist Circular* mean by the term, 'good government'? (*2 marks*)
    c)   Why do these two documents differ so widely in their analysis of the impact of universal suffrage? (*6 marks*)
    d)   Using the knowledge gained from a reading of this chapter, explain why the Chartist campaign for universal suffrage was unsuccessful. (*8 marks*)

4 The Search for Stability 1850–85

POINTS TO CONSIDER

With the rejection of the Third Petition, it was clear that the Chartist challenge had been successfully met. The period from 1850 to 1885 is generally seen by historians as one of social stability and this may seem surprising to anyone familiar with the turmoil of the Chartist years. Trade unions gained a legal status that legitimised their activity and the 'respectable' working class came to support the Liberal and Conservative parties. This raises the issue of whatever happened to the class consciousness that seemed to characterise popular movements in the 1830s and 1840s? In this period, the diversity of the working class is most apparent, as is the desire of working people to work within the social and economic system to maximise their own benefits.

KEY DATES

1851 Great Exhibition; Amalgamated Society of Engineers formed.
1852, 1854, 1859 Government-sponsored Reform Bills rejected by parliament.
1860 Amalgamated Society of Carpenters and Joiners formed.
1865 Birmingham Liberal Association formed under Joseph Chamberlain.
1866 'Sheffield Outrages' raise issue of trade union violence.
1867 Second Reform Act; Royal Commission on Trade Unions; National Union of Conservative and Constitutional Associations formed; first Trade Union Congress held.
1872 Ballot Act.
1874 Election of two 'Lib-Lab' MPs, Alexander Macdonald and Thomas Burt.
1875 Legislation gives trade unions legal status and repeals Master and Servant Act.
1877 National Liberal Federation established.
1883 Corrupt and Illegal Practices Act limits electoral expenses; the Conservatives establish the Primrose League.
1884 Third Reform Act.
1885 Redistribution of Seats Act redraws constituency boundaries.

By 1850 the long campaign for universal suffrage, which had run intermittently since 1815, had clearly failed to achieve its ends. Yet the next phase of popular agitation was marked by some measure of success. By 1875 trade unions had secured full legal status, something they had never previously enjoyed. Besides this, the Second Reform Act of 1867 had conferred the vote on many working men in the towns and the Third Reform Act of 1885 had extended this provision to the rural areas.

To those familiar with the struggles of the Chartist era, these concessions will appear to have been achieved with comparative ease. We may identify three important elements in the broad context from which these changes emerged. Firstly an expansion of the British economy in the period from the mid-1840s onwards. Secondly, the growing realisation on the part of those who held power in mid-Victorian society that the political, economic, and social stability of the nation would be best secured by admitting at least a part of the working class to full citizenship. This was far from being an acceptance of democracy since the corollary to this view was that the less educated, less skilled (and less amenable), part of the working class should still be kept outside what Gladstone called 'the pale of the Constitution'. Thirdly, there was a fundamental shift in the objectives of working-class movements in the period 1850 to 1885.

Although Chartism had never been a revolutionary movement, the granting of the Charter would have had a revolutionary effect on the political structure. The election of large numbers of Chartist MPs, convinced that industrialisation should operate to the benefit of the working community, would have carried profound implications for the social and economic nature of the country. With the end of Chartism working-class radicals seem to have accepted that an industrial society based on competition, and with its characteristic division between capital and labour, had really come to stay. Working-class organisations now aimed, not to change the system, but to adjust it in order to accommodate particular working-class needs. The wide ranging and idealistic aims of Chartism were replaced by demands for rather more limited measures, such as trade union recognition or legal security for friendly society funds. In this period the mass appeal of Chartism was replaced by a more restricted kind of organisation in the form of the mid-Victorian trade unions, which represented no more than 10 per cent of the workforce. The 'labour aristocracy', as the most skilled and best paid sections of the working class have come to be called, argued that they had earned the right to vote and for their unions to be made legal. They no longer invoked their 'natural rights' to back this argument. In contrast to the Chartists they claimed citizenship on the basis of their 'respectability' and generally made their claim through the agency of one of the growing political parties, Liberal or Conservative.

The trade unions of this period adopted a 'reformist' strategy, aiming to reform the system gradually rather than challenging it grandly, as the Chartists had done. They often made their case by using the arguments of the leading economists of the day, accepting the 'laws' of the marketplace. As the trade union journal *The Beehive* put it in 1866: 'it would be wrong to drain from the employers or capitalists more than they can afford to give. It would in the end be injurious to all, because if more capital be absorbed than made, the evil would become general, in general poverty and want'. This certainly made for a less 'heroic' working-class movement. The characteristic activist in this period was not the platform orator but the trade union official. Also, because the main medium for expression was the trade union there could be less representation of the class as a whole. The unions were always primarily concerned with the immediate interests of their members, and it was even possible for one union's interests to be in conflict with those of another. By their very nature unions emphasised the tendency within the working class towards fragmentation, a tendency which had always made Chartist organisation so difficult. In particular, this period saw an increase in the apparent distance between the skilled and the unskilled workers. The broad idea of Chartism as a class movement, struggling for the rights of all workers, was replaced by a more pragmatic yet, it must be said, also a more successful approach. In 1847, Parliament at last passed Fielden's Ten Hours Bill restricting the hours of work in textile factories for women and young persons. This appeared to many to signal a willingness, on the part of those in authority, to carry through social reforms.

As ever, historians are divided in their interpretations of these developments. Among left-wing historians there is a general regret at the passing of Chartism's universal objectives. There is a feeling that the working-class movement 'took a wrong turning' in the period between the end of Chartism and the emergence of the Labour Party at the end of the nineteenth century. In his study of working-class politics in Oldham from 1800 to 1875, John Foster castigates the new union leaders as class traitors for accepting the 'middle-class bribe' of higher wages. Edward Thompson is more realistic, arguing that the limited objectives of trade unionism were all that was achievable in the wake of Chartist defeat: 'the workers, having failed to overthrow capitalist society, proceeded to warren it from end to end'. In his view, after Chartism, the unions established a focus for working-class interests, even though they only directly represented a minority of workers. This point has been developed in the work of Neville Kirk, whose study of trade unions in Lancashire after 1850 suggests that class awareness became focused in trade unions and that these lost none of their energy and resolution.

Liberal historians, on the other hand, tend to see the period's importance as lying in the establishment of a working relationship between capital and labour. In his book, *The Origins of Modern English Society*, Harold Perkin argues that the years after 1850 saw the 'rise of a viable class society' within which conflict could be contained without threatening the overall stability of a society based on competitive individualism. This point has been developed in an influential collection of essays edited by E.F. Biagini and Alistair Reid, *Currents of Radicalism: Popular Radicalism, Organised Labour and Party Politics in*

Britain, 1850–1914 (1991). Here it is argued that working people supported the Liberal and Conservative parties after 1850 because they offered real remedies based on values that could be shared with the middle classes. In particular, Gladstone's free trade budgets in the 1850s and 1860s reduced protective tarrifs on imports, switched taxation away from consumption towards income, and reduced spending on defence. This, alongside his use of public meetings to campaign for his ideas, made him the 'People's William'. Social stability in this period was based on consent and participation, and Chartists like Bronterre O'Brien, Ernest Jones and Robert Lowery found no difficulty in supporting popular Liberalism, because it embraced at least some of the ideas of Chartism.

1 Mid-Victorian Society and the 'Visibility of Progress'

> **KEY ISSUE** What was the relationship between economic development and social stability in the mid-Victorian period?

During the third quarter of the nineteenth century Britain became the 'workshop of the world'. As the first nation to experience an industrial revolution, Britain enjoyed a position of economic pre-eminence. Up to the 1840s, however, this was offset by the vulnerability of its rather immature industrial system to periodic slumps, caused by downturns in the trade cycle. But, from the mid-century, the economy shifted gear and industrial expansion entered a new phase. Most significant was the development of the capital goods sector – those industries requiring large amounts of capital investment, like textiles, coal mining, iron and steel, and shipbuilding. The expansion of these new capital-intensive industries relied heavily on the abilities of the skilled sections of the workforce. Employers became reliant on the skills of the 'respectable working class'.

Economic development was equated invariably with progress and for many people the 'visibility of progress' was epitomised by the Great Exhibition of 1851. Housed in the Crystal Palace, a magnificent prefabricated structure of glass and iron erected in Hyde Park, the Exhibition became the showpiece of the period. Fourteen thousand firms exhibited their wares and over half of these were from Britain and the Empire. Prince Albert opened the exhibition and this royal patronage afforded 'trade' an unprecedented degree of social status. A total of six million visitors attended the exhibition in the next six months. Many of these were working people carried to London by special excursion trains laid on by Thomas Cook in his first venture in the travel trade. The presence of a cross-section of society among the visitors encouraged the optimistic view that the class divisions of the Chartist period were giving way to a society in which values were shared between social groups. *Punch* published its famous cartoon on this theme, 'The Pound and the Shilling', celebrating the fact that the upper and lower classes could be brought together by a visit to the Exhibition. This may have been wishful thinking. In a variety of ways the Exhibition could be said to have epitomised the problems of mid-century society as well as its best aspirations. The trains that carried the visitors to London were rigidly divided into first, second and third class compartments. The Victorians could not even create a transport system without repro-

'The Pound and the Shilling "Whoever Thought of Meeting You Here?"'.
Punch idealistically represents the meeting of the classes at the Great Exhibition; the characters are drawn to represent the middle and upper classes meeting the respectable working class in a spirit of understanding.

ducing the class basis of their society. Similarly, entrance to the Exhibition cost a shilling from Monday to Thursday, two shillings and sixpence on Fridays and five shillings on Saturdays. By avoiding 'shilling days' the upper classes could be certain not to have to mix with working people. The Crystal Palace itself was built of glass and iron to avoid the disputes with the building trade unions that a more permanent structure of bricks and stone would have inevitably involved. However much the mid-Victorian middle class may have wished they lived in a society without social conflict, the differences between the classes did not disappear. Yet social conflict came to be expressed through rather a different framework than had existed previously, and this may be demonstrated by examining the changing legal status of trade unions after 1850.

2 The Legalising of Trade Unions

> **KEY ISSUES** How and why were trade unions able to establish a legal position in this period? Did this limit their activities or their effectiveness in representing their members? For example, if trade unions relied on the law to verify their status, would they be more or less likely to encourage their members to break the law by riotous strike activity? How does this legalisation relate to social stability?

In the space of three-quarters of a century, from 1800 to 1875, trade unions progressed from being illegal organisations, with no rights in law, to legal organisations with a role in the workplace that was widely accepted by employers and employees alike. This dramatic change in their fortunes clearly reflected a significant shift in social attitudes.

a) Ten Pieces of Significant Legislation

i) 1799 and 1800 *The Combination Acts.* Under these Acts any organisation which acted 'in restraint of trade' (for example, by striking, demanding higher wages, or in any way imposing restrictions in the workplace) was deemed illegal. This was not the first piece of legislation to outlaw workers' organisations, but previous Acts had applied to specific trades, such as silkweaving or gunmaking. These new Acts broke new ground by applying to all workers alike. The law also applied to employers' combinations, but in practice these were never prosecuted.

ii) 1813 *Repeal of the Elizabethan Statute of Artificers (1563).* Under Tudor legislation the recruitment to skilled trades was controlled by the regulation of the numbers of apprentices who could be employed at any time. This ensured that skilled work remained highly paid. In addition, magistrates were empowered to set the level of wages in their locality and were entrusted with the task of ensuring that the poor could afford to live. When the Chartists talked of things having been better before industrialisation this was the kind of 'paternal' legislation they had in mind. All of these provisions were repealed in 1813. From now on, it was felt, the 'market' alone should regulate the level of wages and the scale of recruitment to any trade.

iii) 1823 *Master and Servant Act*. This codified previous Master and Servant Acts, and was probably the most significant single piece of trade union legislation before 1875. Under its provisions, employees who broke their contract of work (either written or verbal) could be imprisoned. A strike which resulted in work not being completed could be deemed a breach of contract. Since contracts of work were always two-sided, employers could also be prosecuted (for example, for non-payment of wages), but theirs was a civil and not a criminal offence. They could be fined but not imprisoned. Between 1857 and 1875 (the period for which figures are available) there were on average 10,000 prosecutions of workers per year in England and Wales under the laws relating to master and servant.

iv) 1824 *Repeal of the Combination Acts*. Trade combinations did not disappear with the passing of the Combination Acts. Instead, trade unions seem to have grown in the first quarter of the nineteenth century, but their illegality drove them underground and made them harder to regulate. In 1824 the Combination Acts were repealed in the hope that legality would reduce their attraction to workers and encourage employers to reach agreements with those organisations that continued to exist. The wave of strikes that followed repeal seemed to contradict the logic of this argument.

v) 1825 *An amendment to the repeal of the Combination Acts*. This was a response to the strikes that followed repeal. Trade unions could now legally exist but clause three of this new Act invented a 'new' crime, that of 'molestation'. Unions were forbidden to pressurise fellow workers to join their organisations or their strikes, such pressure constituting 'molestation'. Over the next 50 years courts interpreted this clause fairly loosely – with cases even recorded of fellow workers imprisoned for throwing 'black looks' at non-co-operative fellow workers! After 1825 trade unions were legal but it was difficult to see how a strike could be organised without breaking the law. In 1825, through the operation of this law and the 1823 Master and Servant legislation, the unions entered a period of 'quasi-legality' that lasted until 1875.

vi) 1859 *Molestation of Workmen Act*. This conceded limited rights of picketing, but left it open to the courts to interpret what constituted 'peaceful persuasion'.

vii) 1871 *Trade Union Act*. Registered trade unions were given full legal status including the same legal protection of funds as the Friendly Societies enjoyed.

viii) 1871 *Criminal Law Amendment Act*. This repealed what limited rights to picket trade unions had gained under the Act of 1859. At the time it was widely felt that Gladstone's Liberal government had 'given with one hand only to take with the other' by the two Acts of 1871.

ix) 1875 *Conspiracy and Protection of Property Act.* This made substantial concessions to the unions, by repealing the Criminal Law Amendment Act and legalising peaceful picketing.

x) 1875 *Employers and Workmen Act.* This repealed the earlier Master and Servant legislation. Breach of contract was not now considered a criminal matter and could result only in a fine and not imprisonment.

b) Summary

After 1824 there was never any doubt that trade unions were legal organisations, but until the legislation of 1875 their actions were so circumscribed by law that their legality was largely empty of substance. For most of this period the unions inhabited a twilight world of semi-legality and for this reason the issue of how much freedom or power they should be allowed was hotly debated. For their part, the unions worked hard from the 1840s onwards to achieve legal recognition. There can be no doubt that the gaining of full legal status in 1875 was an enormous achievement, given the hostility to unions that still existed in the country and in Parliament. Yet the achievement carried certain implications for the unions themselves. For legal status to be meaningful, the unions had to be law-abiding bodies. There was no point in acting at variance with the law, say in a strike or lock-out, and then appealing to that same legal framework to verify the unions' own legal status. Put simply, when the unions sought a legally accredited role from the 1840s onwards, they were really agreeing to be bound by the laws of the land.

Also, in order to be protected by the law, unions had to be registered as Friendly Societies. This meant that they became more formal in their organisation than had often been the case before. In the early nineteenth century trade societies had often been loosely-knit groups of workers from one trade in one area. Often without formal rules, they might simply aim to exist for the duration of a particular strike. In the hostile environment of the first half of the century unions rarely survived as organisations for long. They would form at a favourable movement, perhaps in a trade boom like 1833–4, and later disappear when the trade cycle dipped. Thus the emphasis was often more on workers acting together at favourable moments, rather than being members of particular organisations. In studying the building trades, historian Richard Price has argued that before 1850 it was considered more important among workers that they were 'in union' (with one another) than that they were 'in *the* union'. During the 'Plug' strikes of 1842 groups of workers in Lancashire and Yorkshire took over the streets and visited factories, incapacitating them by drawing the boiler plugs. This sort of street-based activity may be seen as an example of this informal and loosely-knit kind of trade organisation. Hundreds of men and women were involved in a boisterous demonstration of feeling that owed much, in terms of its format and organisation, to the traditional food riot. Above all, these informal modes of organisation normally relied on strikes as their first and only weapon.

There were many exceptions to this pattern. In this period many trades aimed at continuity of organisation but found it very difficult in practice. John Doherty created a cotton spinners' union in 1829 which drew workers from Scotland and Lancashire. But the organisation faced major opposition from the employers who provoked two strikes in 1829 and 1837. In 1842 a Miners' Association was formed, drawing together county-based coalmining unions throughout the country. With 70,000 members, it aimed to raise wages by imposing restrictions on coal output, but in 1844 it was broken by a four-month lockout in Northumberland and Durham. During the 1840s national unions were formed among shoemakers, tailors, cotton spinners, glassmakers and printers. All of these initiatives reflect an awareness among trade unionists that their organisations would be stronger if they were bigger. There had always been a willingness to recognise the advantages of amalgamating and federating localised and transient organisations into larger and more permanent bodies. The opportunity to do so came with the expansion of the economy after 1850.

3 The 'Labour Aristocracy' and 'New Model' Unions

> **KEY ISSUES** In what ways were trade unions able to organise in this period to make a successful claim on legal status? To what extent did this involve passive compliance with employers and the State?

As the economy expanded, so the reliance of British industry on skilled labour increased. At the same time increased profitability enabled employers to offer higher wages to the skilled upper stratum of the workforce. Of course, there had always been a hierarchy of skill within the workforce, but the distinctions between the skilled and the unskilled worker now became even more apparent. It has been estimated that, by the 1860s, 14.4 per cent of wage-earners received weekly wages at 40–50 per cent above those of common labourers. This 'labour aristocracy' consisted of workers in the growing primary industries (engineers, boilermakers, miners, cotton spinners, shipbuilders, etc.), and the most skilled sectors of the traditional industries (shoemakers, the building trades, etc.). This was the section of the working class that could afford to belong to Friendly Societies as an insurance against bad times and personal misfortune. They also formed the backbone of the co-operative stores that flourished throughout the country in the second half of the nineteenth century. These were founded and run by working people and enabled subscribing members to buy unadulterated goods at sensible prices. The development of trade union organisation in this period emphasised the diversity of the working class and the distance between the skilled and the unskilled worker.

Because of the importance of their skills to a growing economy the skilled trades were in a good position to organise themselves. From the late 1840s large federated unions appeared in many of these trades. In 1851 the Amalgamated Society of Engineers was formed as a national union with a highly centralised structure that was run by full-time salaried officials. By 1867 the ASE had 33,300 members, 308 branches and financial reserves of £140,000. The Amalgamated Society of Carpenters and Joiners (ASCJ), formed in 1860, was a federation of 230 branches by 1867. In 1894, in the first real history of trade unionism to be written, the historians Sidney and Beatrice Webb referred to such organisations as 'New Model' unions. In a sense this is a misleading term since there was little about the 'new model' that was actually new. Unions had been attempting to establish themselves as large permanent organisations for many years. Most of the new unions were simply revitalised versions of established, though less secure, organisations. Thus the United Flint Glass Makers Society was first formed in 1844, but it revised its rules and re-organised its structure along 'new model' lines in 1858. The ASE itself was formed from the amalgamation of a number of existing trade societies for engineering workers. Three quarters of the membership of the ASE at its inception came from the Society of Journeymen Steam Engine Makers which had been in existence since 1826.

The 'new model' unions also inherited much of their organisation and strategy from earlier unions. For example, they emphasised their role as Friendly Societies and aimed to provide sickness and unemployment benefits. Unions had always attempted to do this, although never with great success. But the 'new model' unions adopted a very systematic approach to benefit provision. They charged high subscription rates (around a shilling a week), and used this money to build up a reliable fund for their members. From 1875 to 1879 the ASE paid out £350,000 in unemployment benefit. Even the idea of paid full-time officials was not a new departure. The stonemasons had applied this in 1834, as had the miners in 1842. All that was really new about the 'new model' unions was their effectiveness in applying these strategies and their ultimate success in persuading employers of their acceptability.

The aim of the amalgamated societies was to improve conditions for their members by restricting entry to the trade and ensuring that work was spread evenly. They invariably resisted the employment of unskilled labour, insisting on the use of skilled union men for particular jobs. They also opposed the use by employers of systematic overtime and piecework (payment by the amount of work completed), both of which tended to increase the pressure on the individual worker to be more productive, and thus decrease the total amount of work available.

The key to the success of the new model unions lay in two factors. First, the importance of skilled workers to the industrial expansion from the late 1840s through which Britain emerged as the 'workshop of the world'. This gave the skilled unions the kind of leverage on employers that they had never really possessed before. Second, they chose to apply this leverage via a strategy of negotiation rather than direct action in the form of strikes. The Webbs characterised this as the 'new spirit' of those trade unions initiated in the 1850s. It became apparent that such a strategy was likely to bring better results than confrontation.

Sometimes this lesson was learned the hard way. In 1852 the ASE found itself involved in a costly dispute in Lancashire which quickly spread to other areas. The unity of the employers defeated the union and the dispute cost the ASE £40,000 in strike pay. If the unions were to secure their permanent existence such costly strikes would have to be avoided. As Robert Applegarth, General Secretary of the ASCJ, put it to his members: 'Never surrender the right to strike, but be careful how you use a double edged weapon.' George Odger of the shoemakers was similarly circumspect about direct action: 'Strikes in the social world are like wars in the political world: both are crimes unless justified by absolute necessity.' Increasingly, employers and unions opted to settle disputes by the use of an agreed third party as an arbitrator. Strikes certainly did not disappear in this period, but they were no longer seen as a union's first weapon.

The centralisation of union organisation helped to enforce this strategy. In most of the 'new model' unions the permission of the central Executive Council was needed before a strike could take place. The 'new model' aimed at a national organisation but it was often adopted by trades based in one region. The East Lancashire Power Loom Weavers' Association was formed in 1858. It put the powers of negotiation and decision-making in the hands of district committees, as part of a centralised structure. Such devices made it easier to control militant workers on the shop floor and to encourage a policy of moderation. This spirit of conciliation was reflected in the public image of the new model unions. The membership certificate of the ASE, for example, celebrated the importance of the respectable workman in the creation of a rational and civilised society (see page 86).

Local trade union activity in most of the large towns was co-ordinated by Trades' Councils. The first of these was formed in Liverpool in 1848 and the example was soon followed throughout the country.

The London Trades' Council, formed in 1860, drew together an influential group whom the Webbs, in their history, called the 'Junta': William Allen of the ASE, Applegarth of the ASCJ, Daniel Guile of the Ironfounders, Edwin Coulson of the Bricklayers and George Odger of the Shoemakers. Great public concern was created, in 1866, by a series of violent attacks, in Sheffield, by saw-grinders on fellow-workers who refused to be bound by their local union (the so-called Sheffield 'Outrages'). As a result, a Royal Commission was appointed to investigate the role of trade unions generally. The 'Junta' co-ordinated and presented the evidence on behalf of the unions. Their condemnation of the 'Outrages' as an unacceptable approach to industrial relations and their stress on 'respectable' and conciliatory trade unionism had much to do with the subsequent shift in government policy towards legalising the unions. The issue of legal status became particularly pressing for the unions themselves in 1867 following the Hornby v Close judgement. The Boilermakers' Union attempted to sue a dishonest official but a court decided that union funds were in fact not protected by the Friendly Societies' legislation. In effect this meant that trade union funds were not protected by law. This only served to emphasise the continuing vulnerability of unions as a result of their indeterminate legal position.

The 'Junta' saw themselves as the self-nominated national spokesmen for the unions and this caused some resentment. Despite the growth of the amalgamated societies, the older union tradition of small highly localised trade clubs lived on throughout the country. These, frequently more militant, organisations were co-ordinated by the Trades' Councils in many areas. In London George Potter ran the General Union of Carpenters as a local alternative to the ASCJ. His newspaper, the *Beehive*, ran from 1861 to 1876. It had a national circulation among trade unionists and tended to reject the moderate strategies of the 'new model' Junta. So the large amalgamated societies were not the only unions fighting to change the labour laws. In 1863 the Glasgow Trades' Council initiated a nationwide campaign against the Master and Servant legislation. Inspired by the promising nature of this movement, in 1867 the Manchester Trades' Council sent out invitations for a 'Congress of Trade Unions' that would argue the union case nationally. At first the 'Junta' held aloof, fearing that the new organisation would undermine their own push for union legality. Thirty-four delegates attended the first Trade Union Congress (TUC), representing 118, 367 members. However, the passing of the Criminal Law Amendment Act of 1871, with its punitive restrictions on picketing, tended to draw the trade union leadership together, and the TUC became the focus of a united campaign to repeal the Act. In 1873 the old Chartist days were recalled when 100,000 trade unionists met in Hyde Park to call for repeal.

The ultimate success of 'respectable' unionism, in achieving legality by 1875, should not lead us to think that trade unions were passive

Membership certificate of the ASE; the imagery presents the skilled working
class as it wished to be seen: respectable, significant and purposeful.

organisations or that they were always positively welcomed by those in
authority in the mid-Victorian period. Charles Dickens' fictional
depiction of the union leader 'Slackbridge' in his novel *Hard Times,*
published in 1854, was aimed at a middle-class audience that shared
his view of the unions as a threat to stability. Dickens had visited
Preston in 1853 when 26,000 cotton spinners were locked out for 28

weeks by employers who refused to recognise their union. In Dickens' novel Slackbridge addresses a union meeting:

1 'Oh my friends, the down-trodden operatives of Coketown! Oh my friends and fellow-countrymen, the slaves of an iron-handed and a grinding despotism! Oh my friends and fellow-sufferers, and fellow-workmen, and fellow-men!' ... As he stood there, trying to quench his 5 fiery face with his drink of water, the comparison between the orator and the crowd of attentive faces turned towards him, was extremely to his disadvantage ... He was not so honest, he was not so manly, he was not so good humoured; he substituted cunning for their simplicity, and passion for their safe solid sense.

Many of the employers giving evidence to the 1867 Royal Commission on trade unions expressed precisely this view of the union leaders. As far as a middle class committed to the free market were concerned, the unions interfered with economic freedom and kept both wages and prices artificially high. This led them to question the morality of the trade unionists. Yet there was little of 'Slackbridge' in any of the answers given patiently by the carpenters' leader, Robert Applegarth, to the 633 questions put to him by the Royal Commission. Similarly, Allen of the ASE emphasised the unions' concern with the morality of their members:

1 I think it [the union] has been of decided improvement in them in their position and character generally; for we have a controlling power over them; if men misconduct themselves through drinking or anything of that kind, we have the opportunity of dealing with them, and we do our 5 best to keep them up to the mark so far as regards their position.

For Dickens the union leadership embodied all that was bad in the working community. As far as union leaders, such as Applegarth and Allen, were concerned, they embodied all that was good. The debate over the unions continued despite the legislation passed by Disraeli's Conservative government in 1875. The establishment of a National Agricultural Labourers' Union in 1872 signalled that trade unionism would not remain the preserve of the skilled 'labour aristocracy' for long. As the next chapter will show, once the less skilled began to unionise themselves in the 1880s the whole issue of union legality was opened up once again.

For the time being, legalising the unions was the kind of gamble that appealed to a political opportunist like Disraeli. It would, it was hoped, encourage 'respectable' craft unions with their moderate policies and high subscription rates. This would emphasise the distinctions within the working class by conferring benefits on one section of that class. The same strategy lay behind the decision in 1867 to extend the vote to some working men.

4 The Reform Act of 1867

> **KEY ISSUES** Why was a section of the working class admitted to the franchise in 1867? How important was popular pressure in the passing of the Second Reform Act?

a) Pressure for Reform

The Reform Act of 1832 left the industrial middle class largely unsatisfied, yet their fear of a full democratisation of the franchise prevented them from supporting Chartism. With the demise of Chartism, however, the idea of a franchise extension which would serve their needs was revived. Middle-class radicalism drew its strength from a combination of commercial considerations and nonconformist religious fervour. Middle-class radicals sought free trade, educational reform, religious equality between Anglicans and Nonconformists and a control of public spending that would keep down rates and taxes. The costly, and often disastrous, conduct of the Crimean War (1854–6) epitomised for many the inefficiencies of aristocratic government. When John Bright was returned to Parliament for Birmingham in 1857, he began a national agitation for parliamentary reform. In 1864 he formed the National Reform Union, a middle-class organisation which aimed at household suffrage, the ballot, and a redistribution of seats to favour the urban boroughs. Bright became convinced that the skilled working class, if enfranchised, would back the middle class against the aristocracy.

In fact, social attitudes to the working class had shifted perceptibly by the late 1850s. It was common for commentators to make distinctions between the 'rough' and the 'respectable' working man. The involvement of the skilled working class in co-operatives and friendly societies seemed to be an endorsement of the values of thrift and sobriety by which the middle class tried to order their own lives. In the practical day-to-day administration of the Poor Law, overseers often distinguished between the 'deserving' and the 'undeserving' poor, prescribing out-relief for the former and the workhouse for the latter. Although suspicion and hostility toward trade unions continued, middle-class fear of the working class was now focused on the 'undeserving' poor, sometimes called the 'dangerous classes' or the 'residuum'.

For their part, trade unionists saw the franchise as an important element in achieving changes in the labour laws. The revival of working-class politics was encouraged by the unification struggles in Italy in 1859, the Polish revolt of 1863, and the American Civil War of 1861–5, all of which were followed with intense interest in Britain. In 1865 the Working Men's Garibaldi Committee (formed to welcome the Italian on a visit to London) became the basis of a new reform organisation, called the Reform League.

The Reform League was committed to universal suffrage. But, mindful of the lessons of Chartism, the League made it clear from the outset that it would happily co-operate with Bright's Reform Union to achieve a more limited measure. Even its version of universal suffrage was more limited than that of the Chartists. The Reform League accepted the view of the middle-class reformers that only workmen who were 'registered and residential' should have the vote. Under the Reform Act of 1832 it was necessary for men who qualified for the franchise to register their names in the constituency in which they lived. Registration was dependent upon a residence qualification of a year. Limiting the vote to 'registered and residential' working men would exclude a large section of the working class who were either of no fixed abode or who frequently changed localities in pursuit of work. At each new address they would have to establish a new residence qualification. Middle-class reformers were convinced that a 'registered and residential' franchise would exclude the 'dangerous classes' from the vote. The trade unions saw such a measure reaffirming the role of the aristocracy of labour. The League, with the bricklayers' moderate leader George Howell as its Secretary, was widely supported by trade unionists, particularly the London based 'Junta'.

In Parliament it was widely accepted by the 1860s that reform was unavoidable. The issue now was the form that it would take. The political parties had undergone considerable change since the days of the Chartists. In 1846 Peel had split the Tories over Corn Law repeal and we may date the emergence of the Conservative Party from the internal wranglings that followed. The Whigs, who had forced through reform in 1832, found themselves challenged in their own party by the Liberals who recognised a need to draw the nonconformist middle class into an active political alliance. Liberals, such as Bright and Cobden, seemed to represent the new age and even Lord John Russell accepted the need to broaden the aristocratic base of the old Whig connection to include the new men. In 1838 his anti-reform 'finality' declaration had done much to stiffen Chartist resolve, yet in 1851 he expressed his fears that social stability could not be guaranteed unless 'the sound morals and the clear intelligence of the best of the working classes' were drawn into the political nation. It was said at the time that 'Finality Jack' had become 'Fidgety John'.

The debate over parliamentary reform focused on the related questions of the franchise and the redistribution of seats. Both parties were agreed that universal suffrage was undesirable and that the vote should remain linked, in some way, to the possession of property. Some sort of household suffrage was the obvious solution, but this was by no means straightforward. Should the 1832 £10 borough franchise simply be lowered a few pounds to allow in more voters? Should the vote accrue to all who *owned* a house or, more radically, to all who *occupied* a house? An occupier franchise might still be restricted by two devices. First, by imposing a residence qualification which must be met before a person could register for the vote, and second, by including only occupants who paid their local rates personally. This would exclude 'compounders', people who simply paid rent to a landlord who, in return, retained responsibility for the payment of rates. About two-thirds of householders were compounders, so this would be a considerable restriction. Of course, compounders still paid rates but they did so indirectly (the landlord recovering his payment via the rent he charged to tenants). It was the rate payer, it was argued, who had the stake in the country and this should be reflected in the franchise.

Redistribution was an equally fraught parliamentary issue as it became increasingly clear that the parties drew strength from different geographical areas. The Conservatives wanted the county vote bolstered whilst the Liberals were just as keen to redistribute seats to the growing boroughs.

Government-sponsored Reform Bills were rejected by Parliament in 1852, 1854 and 1859. Each was backed by either minority governments or those with the smallest of majorities. Further debate on the subject was blocked in the early 1860s by Palmerston, the anti-reform leader of the Liberals. His death in 1865 and the election of a Liberal government under Russell, with a working majority of 70 seats, seemed to open up the issue again. Russell and Gladstone drew up a Reform Bill in 1866 which proposed to lower the £10 householder franchise in the boroughs to £7, and to extend the county franchise to tenants paying an annual rent of £14.

The rather limited nature of this proposal, from two recognised advocates of reform, is a reminder that there was never any intention to 'democratise' the nation. Yet the Liberal Party had gained considerable support from the skilled working class in the 1850s and 1860s, particularly encouraged by the Liberals' emphasis on free trade, and the importance of local government and minimal state intervention. Gladstone, the architect of the bill, wanted to construct a new voting system that would not rock the constitutional boat, whilst at the same time conferring the benefits of any new voting power on the Liberal Party. The £7 franchise, he calculated, would enfranchise educated working-class men in the boroughs, and he believed that they would vote Liberal. But the Bill gave rise to a revolt in his own party by the traditional Whigs, led by the Liberal Robert Lowe. This group was dubbed the 'Adullamites' by Bright, a reference to the Old Testament story of David who hid from Saul in the 'cave Adullam' and gathered discontents around him. Lowe, a follower of Bentham, argued that 'people' were not entitled to the vote, only to 'good government'. He scorned Gladstone's claim that the working classes had 'improved'. Instead he presented a re-working of the old 'swinish multitude' theme, which was always guaranteed to raise some support in the Commons.

The alliance of the Whigs and the Conservatives was enough to end the Liberal initiative. A Redistribution Bill was defeated by 11 votes in

June 1866. Russell resigned and a minority Conservative government was formed under Lord Derby with Disraeli leading the government in the Commons. Despite their opposition to the Liberals' measure, Derby's administration had, within a year of taking office, forced through their own Reform Act. This was designed by Disraeli and, in its final form, it admitted fully three times more new voters than the Liberals had envisaged in their proposed measure.

Disraeli's Reform Bill, introduced in March 1867, had originally opted for household suffrage in the boroughs limited to personal payers of rates who fulfilled a two-year residence qualification. The 400,000 new voters to be created would have been roughly comparable to the number enfranchised under Gladstone's Bill of the previous year. Yet, in the process of parliamentary debate, Disraeli accepted amendments that greatly increased the number of new voters. One of these gave the vote to lodgers in the boroughs whose rent exceeded £10 per year. Also accepted was an amendment to include compounders in the borough franchise. In addition, the residence qualification was cut to a year. As a result the Reform Act of 1867 introduced a generous version of household suffrage to the boroughs. In the counties the vote was extended to occupiers of property rated at £12 per year or more. The enfranchisement of nearly one and a quarter million new voters was described even by Lord Derby as a 'leap in the dark'.

b) Labour and the 'Hyde Park Rail-Way' to Reform

It has been argued by the left-wing historian Royden Harrison that Disraeli's hand was forced by the agitation outside Parliament led by the Reform League. The rejection of the Liberal Bill in June 1866 was followed in early July by a series of huge reform demonstrations in Trafalgar Square. When the Reform League called a rally in Hyde Park later in the month they found themselves shut out by the Metropolitan Police, under orders from the Home Secretary. The crowd, incensed at what was seen as an infringement of free speech, tore down the railings around the Park to gain entry. Three nights of rioting followed and order was only restored by the intervention of the leaders of the Reform League who appealed for calm.

That winter brought a cholera epidemic and a downturn in trade. The Hornby v Close decision and the calling of a Royal Commission on trade unions after an outburst of violence against non-union labour in the Sheffield metal-working trades (the Sheffield 'Outrages') only served to aggravate the situation. A government backlash against the unions seemed a likely response, and union leaders were more concerned than ever to secure legal status for their organisations. When Disraeli introduced his Bill in February 1867 the situation in the country was already extremely tense. His privately declared intention was 'to destroy the present agitation and to extinguish Gladstone and Co'.

The government banned a subsequent rally planned for 6 May. Comparisons with the Chartist rally of 10 April 1848 were drawn by contemporaries, and certainly the government prepared in a similar way on both occasions. Fifteen thousand special constables were enrolled and both the police and the army were placed on alert. At 6pm on 6 May the Reform League entered Hyde Park unopposed at the head of a procession of 100,000 people. They marched behind a red flag topped by a Cap of Liberty. The imagery was important. The Cap of Liberty was a symbol of the French Revolution that had been much used by the Chartists. The red flag was the emblem of the new socialist International Working Men's Association. This had been formed in London in 1864 by Karl Marx, and it included in its ranks a large number of trade unionists, among them Robert Applegarth and George Odger, both members of the 'Junta'. The International, as it became known, aimed to unite labour representatives across Europe so that united action and support would be possible.

The demonstration of 6 May seemed to present the government with a clear choice: enfranchise the 'respectable' working class or they would return to the mass politics of the Chartist days, and be drawn into the orbit of European socialist movements. The meeting was held without disorder, but the fact that it went ahead despite the ban was seen at the time as a humiliation for the Government. The Home Secretary, Horace Walpole, did the decent thing and resigned. Only 11 days after the meeting, Disraeli accepted the amendment admitting compounders. This trebled the number of voters contemplated in Disraeli's original Bill. Royden Harrison believes this can be attributed to the Government's fear of popular disorder.

However, the view that an apprehensive Disraeli took what *Punch* referred to as the 'Hyde Park Rail-Way' to reform, has been widely contested. Maurice Cowling makes the point that whilst it is clear that the popular agitation kept parliamentary reform high on the political agenda, the form the Act eventually took reflected the parliamentary struggle between the parties rather than the feeling of the country. Disraeli's biographer, the Conservative historian Robert Blake, has argued that Disraeli was motivated by two concerns. One was to demonstrate that the new Conservative Party, which had been in opposition since 1846, could 'move with the times' and pass a popular measure. The other concern was that the Conservatives should have a hand in any redistribution of seats that accompanied reform of the franchise.

Above all, Disraeli aimed to maintain Conservative strength in the counties. In fact, he eventually had to compromise a little and agree to third members for Liverpool, Manchester, Birmingham and Leeds, and a second for Salford and Merthyr. But 25 new county seats were finally created and when the Act was extended to Scotland the following year, three further county seats were added there. During the passage of the Act, Disraeli showed himself to be willing to accept amendments that appeared to alter the shape of his measure significantly. Yet his acceptance of such amendments was always carefully calculated. Take, for example, two that he opposed successfully. One proposed that the words 'adult males' be replaced by 'adult persons', thus admitting women. Disraeli also opposed an amendment which called for election expenses to be paid from the rates, believing that this would encourage the growth of an independent party representing labour. On the other hand, he was not too concerned at amendments that increased the number of borough voters since this would not alter the balance of power. He shared Gladstone's view that the urban working class would mostly vote Liberal. Rather than upsetting the status quo between Liberals and Conservatives, this would simply create more urban voters in what were already Liberal constituencies.

Whilst analogies with 1832 are probably misplaced, since 1867 was not a revolutionary situation, it is equally clear that the agitation in the country had an effect on the deliberations in Westminster. In introducing parliamentary reform in 1866 Gladstone expressed the hope that the House of Commons would be 'wise in time'. As we have seen, Disraeli's privately declared intention was to outmanoeuvre Gladstone in Parliament and the popular reformers in the country. Thus it seems appropriate to see the Act as both a response to public opinion as well as a piece of expert parliamentary footwork on the part of Disraeli. To have orchestrated a Reform Act which served the ends of the Conservatives whilst operating as part of a minority government was an enormous parliamentary achievement. Although ousted in the election that immediately followed the Act, the Conservatives were returned with a majority of 32 seats in 1874 and with Disraeli as Prime Minister.

5 The Development of Modern Party Structures

> **KEY ISSUE** How did the political parties adapt to embrace working-class voters?

The Reform Act of 1867 ushered in the age of mass politics. In England, Wales and Scotland one adult male in every three now had the right to vote (one in six in Ireland). This inevitably carried implications for the way politics were conducted. For example, it no longer seemed prudent to conduct elections in the boisterous style the Victorians had inherited from the eighteenth century. Voting was a public affair and this often degenerated into riot as parties sought to exert undue influence on the voters. After a by-election in Rochdale in 1865 John Bright confided to his diary that: 'The town was very excited all the week; much fighting and drinking – as usual under our system of elections.' This seemed at odds with the otherwise demure style of Victorian public life, and was also a major threat to public order in the growing cities. When Gladstone's Liberal administration introduced the secret ballot in 1872 to rectify this abuse there was little opposition. Yet the large-scale buying and selling of votes remained common and the election of 1880 was said to have been the most expensive in British history. In response the Corrupt and Illegal Practices Prevention Act of 1883 prescribed a limit to the election expenses that a candidate could incur.

After 1867 it became increasingly clear that it was neither possible nor desirable for a mass electorate to be bought or cajoled in the traditional eighteenth-century style. Rather, it now had to be persuaded. This, and the limit on election expenses, meant that candidates needed to be backed by an effective party machinery crewed by enthusiastic volunteers. So, with the extension of the electorate, both major parties began to consolidate and extend their organisations throughout the country. In 1867 the National Union of Conservative and Constitutional Associations was formed and in 1877 the National Liberal Federation was established. Both these organisations worked hard to attract the new working-class voters and their success was the despair of European revolutionary observers. 'Everywhere the proletariat are the tag, rag and bobtail of the official parties', wrote Engels despairingly to Marx in 1868.

The Liberals were particularly successful in the boroughs, where their organisations were modelled on the Birmingham Liberal Association. This was established in 1865 and aimed to draw working men into the same organisation as middle-class voters. Its most celebrated leader was the screw-manufacturer Joseph Chamberlain who, as Birmingham's mayor from 1873 to 1876 and then one of the city's MPs, piloted social reforms calculated to bring the classes together. The council took over responsibility for the city's water and gas supply, and set to work clearing slum areas. Through an intricate local party structure, called a 'caucus', the Liberals ensured that no Conservative was elected for Birmingham between 1867 and 1885. The 'caucus' was radical in politics and Nonconformist in religion, and Chamberlain's strategy was to emphasise those areas that the classes had in common. When he established the National Liberal Federation in 1877, he applied similar principles to the party as a whole. Above all, he recognised the need to allow some working-class participation in organising and running the party machine, at least at a local level.

The Liberals even accepted that a few constituencies might be represented by working men standing under the auspices of the Liberal Party. 1874 saw the election of two working-class Liberals (or 'Lib-Lab's as they were called). These were both trade unionists and miners: Alexander Macdonald elected for Stafford and Thomas Burt for Morpeth.

As a result, by the late 1870s the Liberal Party had become the party with which the working-class voter identified himself in most urban constituencies. Liberal success in the general election of 1880 led the Conservatives to reorganise their party network. In 1883 they established the Primrose League as a social and political organisation geared to engendering and maintaining party support. It was particularly successful in drawing the middle class and the 'aristocracy of labour' together in the small market towns where Conservative support was strong. It also mobilised women (the Primrose Dames), and even children (the Primrose Buds).

By the 1880s the existence of a mass electorate was accepted as a fact of life. The admission of the working-class voter, with the safeguard that this was restricted to 'registered and residential' men, was seen as a social stabiliser giving the best of the workforce a 'stake in the country'. For this reason the Reform Act of 1884, introduced by Gladstone, was not seen in Parliament as a particularly contentious issue. It used the borough franchise of 1867 as a basis for creating a uniform franchise in county and borough alike throughout the United Kingdom. Thus the vote was given to householders and lodgers in the counties who fulfilled a one year's residence qualification. Two and a half million new voters were created in this way.

Gladstone and the new Conservative leader Lord Salisbury agreed between themselves the redrawing of constituency boundaries. This was enshrined in the Redistribution of Seats Act of 1885. The party leaders opted for mostly single member constituencies of roughly equal size. Although Salisbury was from an established landed family, he was aware that support for the Conservatives was broadening. Alongside the county interest which Disraeli had been so keen to protect in 1867, there were Conservative voters to be found in the new lower middle-class suburbs springing up around the large towns. In the process of redistribution Salisbury was careful to separate these areas from the predominantly Liberal-voting working-class areas. As a result, class became a more important determinant of voting behaviour and of the pattern of results than had ever been the case before. The story that Salisbury prevented the elderly Gladstone from seeing the re-drawn constituency map the right way up during their private meeting, is no doubt apocryphal. Nevertheless, this redistribution ensured the continuing electoral resilience of the Conservatives into the twentieth century.

Gladstone's biographer E.J. Feuchtwanger argues that: 'the third Reform Bill moved the country almost all the way towards political democracy'. This is not a very accurate appreciation of a political system that, despite the changes, still only included 28.5 per cent of all adults (male and female) and which remained heavily distorted against the interests of labour. Women were still not enfranchised and parliamentary motions to give them the vote were rejected in every parliamentary session between 1870 and 1885. Under the 1884 Act men who owned houses in more than one borough or county constituency could exercise more than one vote. Needless to say, plural voters were not generally working-class voters. Men in receipt of poor relief were disenfranchised; these were generally working-class voters. Also the one year's residential qualification (compounded by the delay involved in getting onto the register once this qualification had been met) disenfranchised many working-class men. It seems unlikely that before 1918 more than 6 men in every 10 were ever actually in a position to exercise the vote. Nor, we should remember, was this an unfortunate by-product of badly devised legislation. It had been accepted in 1867 and 1884 that residential qualifications and voter registration were useful devices to restrict working-class participation. In 1912 the conservative MP Sir William Anson defended the principle of plural voting to the Commons in a way that Edmund Burke would have accepted:

> Is the man who is too illiterate to read his ballot paper, who is too imprudent to support his children, to be placed on the same footing as the man who by industry and capacity has acquired a substantial interest in more than one constituency?

But this was a strategy that backfired. The political system appeared democratic yet, in practice, it was heavily distorted against the working community. Shut out from effective political participation, labour returned to traditional forms of direct action in the late 1880s. Industrial relations assumed a renewed bitterness in the 30 years that followed the Third Reform Act. The same period also saw the emergence of an independent working-class political party.

Working on Chapter 4

After the apparent turmoil of the Chartist years the third quarter of the century seems relatively calm. In making notes on this period you need to capture the idea that successive governments were attempting to provide a political and social framework that would produce stability. There were always two sides to this. Too little political reform would encourage a revival of radicalism but too much would itself threaten the social fabric. The reforms of these years were a political balancing act and whilst you are observing how much things were changing you should also be aware of how much remained the same. Be careful, for example, to identify who was being included and who excluded from the changes.

While you are taking detailed notes to help you to establish the sequence of events, you may find it useful to keep available two sheets of paper on which to collect answers to the two questions that are central to the chapter:

1. Why legalise trade unions in the 1870s?
2. Why extend the franchise in 1867 and 1884?

Summary Diagram
The Search for Stability 1850–85

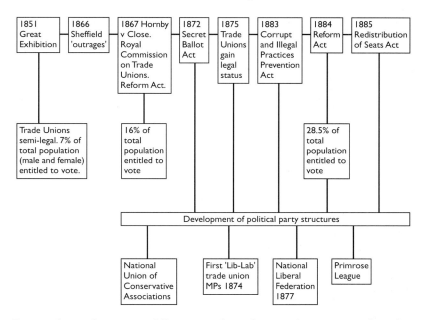

| 1851 Great Exhibition | 1866 Sheffield 'outrages' | 1867 Hornby v Close. Royal Commission on Trade Unions. Reform Act. | 1872 Secret Ballot Act | 1875 Trade Unions gain legal status | 1883 Corrupt and Illegal Practices Prevention Act | 1884 Reform Act | 1885 Redistribution of Seats Act |

Trade Unions semi-legal. 7% of total population (male and female) entitled to vote.

16% of total population entitled to vote

28.5% of total population entitled to vote

Development of political party structures

National Union of Conservative Associations

First 'Lib-Lab' trade union MPs 1874

National Liberal Federation 1877

Primrose League

Remember, when assembling your thoughts on these two topics, that there are a variety of viewpoints to be considered. For example, Bright or Gladstone would answer the questions differently from William Allen of the ASE. Use the chapter to tease out the different contemporary perspectives on these issues. You should expect to find a number of different answers to the questions.

Answering structured and essay questions on Chapter 4

The framework for many questions in this area is provided by the shift from social instability in the 1830s and 1840s to the apparent stability of the mid-Victorian period; from illegal unions and non-voting workers in 1850 to legal unions and working-class voters by 1885, from apparent class solidarity in the 1840s to the social diversity of the mid-Victorian period. A structured question on this topic will ask you to build your answer.

a) How important were the skills of the workforce in the period after 1850? (*5 marks*)
b) How did the legal status of trade unions change after 1850? (*5 marks*)
c) What was new about the 'new model unions' that emerged in the period 1850–1875? (*10 marks*)

Here the increased social stability of the mid-Victorian period can be related to changes in the economy emphasising the role of skill, and the way this was embodied in the organisation and legal status of trade unions. This was reflected in a new form of organisation, which was designed to be effective in this new context.

Essay questions on these topics will test your ability to explain the process of *change through time*. To answer effectively you must develop the skill of presenting an *analytical narrative*.

Here are some typical questions on the topics covered by this chapter:

1. How and why did the nature of trade unionism change between 1833 and 1875?
2. Comment on developments in trade union organisation and policies between 1824 and 1871.
3. Identify and explain the main successes and failures of British working-class movements from 1833 to 1875.
4. Given the supposed finality of the 1832 Reform Act, why did further reform of Parliament come about in 1867?

Each of these questions presents you with a precise chronological framework for your answer. None of these dates has been chosen at random, each of them sounds a keynote for your response. Thus, question 2 takes you from the GNCTU of 1833, which engendered such a hostile government response the following year, through to the legislation of 1875 which gave the unions a substantial legal status for the first time. Your first task, therefore, is to establish the exact nature of the change through the time span involved in each of these questions.

Having done this you can turn to the issue of causation. Ask yourself, 'what were the long-term and short-term causes of change?' In establishing long-term causes remember that this was a period of intense social and economic development. What were the major social and economic shifts evident in the period defined by the chronology and how did these bear on the topic specified by the question? It is often easier to establish the short-term causes of change because of their immediate proximity to the events under scrutiny. Nevertheless, a full answer will relate long-term influences to short-term causes. For example, question 4 operates clearly on two levels: 'why a further reform?' but also, 'why reform in 1867?' Disraeli's desire to establish Conservative credibility by piloting the 1867 Reform Act through at almost any cost was clearly a significant factor behind reform, but what were the broader social and economic factors that created the *context* within which Disraeli's opportunism operated? Alongside the important political influences, you will need to look at the development of the labour aristocracy as a result of economic change, moderate trade unionism, fear of the 'residuum' etc. Similarly, in the essays dealing with changes in trade unions an event such as, for example, the Hornby v Close judgement was clearly a very important moment in the unions' push for legality. But you need to establish the social and economic factors that gave the moment its significance. Without this wider context the story cannot be unfolded properly and the revelation of 'what happened next' will lose its impact.

Source-based questions on Chapter 4

1. Hard Times and the Royal Commission on Trade Unions, 1867

Compare the extract from *Hard Times* and the statement by William Allen of the ASE on page 87. Answer the following questions:

a) What is Dickens' purpose in making Slackbridge use the word 'fellow' so much in his speech? (*3 marks*)

b) Compare and contrast the different views of trade unions expressed in the two extracts. (*6 marks*)

c) Relate these views to the decisions to legalise trade unions in 1875, and to extend the franchise in 1867 and 1884. (*6 marks*)

5 The Development of the Labour Party 1885–1902

POINTS TO CONSIDER

In the mid-Victorian period trade unions worked hard to establish their legal status, whilst skilled workers generally stressed their 'respectability' in a way that was acceptable to the middle class. In contrast, the last 15 years of the nineteenth century saw the re-birth of militant trade unionism and the emergence of an independent working-class political party. The key points to consider here are: where did this new initiative come from and how was the infant Labour Party influenced by the circumstances of its birth? Remember, the Labour Party grew from a background of Liberalism and moderate trade unionism and this shaped its commitment to 'reformism'.

KEY DATES

1879 Henry George publishes *Poverty and Progress*.

1884 Social Democratic Federation (SDF), Socialist League and Fabian Society established.

1885 Two SDF candidates stand for London constituencies in a general election and poll 59 votes between them.

1886 Eight Hours League established by Tom Mann; Henry Broadhurst, Secretary of TUC, made Under Secretary to the Home Office and becomes first working man to hold government office.

1887 First edition of Karl Marx's *Das Kapital* appears in English. November – 'Bloody Sunday' in Trafalgar Square.

1888 July – strike at Bryant and May's matchworks, East London, by female workforce; Keir Hardie forms Scottish Labour Party.

1889 Strike at East Ham gasworks, led by Will Thorne; strike by dockers led by Ben Tillett who now forms the Dock, Wharf, Riverside and General Labourers' Union; General Railway Workers' Union formed; Miners' Federation of Great Britain formed.

1890 Shipping Federation formed by employers.

1891 Federation of Master Cotton Spinners formed; Manningham Mills strike in Yorkshire.

1892 Hardie, Burns and Havelock-Wilson elected as independent labour candidates in general election.

1893 Formation of William Collison's National Free Labour Association to provide strike-breaking workers; (July–November) lock-out by coal owners in Lancashire, Yorkshire and the Midlands; two miners killed in clashes with troops in Featherstone, Yorkshire; the

Independent Labour Party (ILP) formed following a conference in Bradford.

1895 All 28 ILP candidates defeated at the general election.

1896 Conciliation Act passed, conciliators could be appointed by the Board of Trade in the event of a dispute; Engineering Employers' Federation formed.

1897 Lock-out of engineering workers demanding an eight-hour day.

1898 Formation of Employers' Federation Parliamentary Committee.

1900 Formation of Labour Representation Committee.

1901 Taff Vale judgement in House of Lords.

1 The Late-Victorian Social Crisis

> **KEY ISSUE** What social and economic factors, in the last two decades of the nineteenth century, encouraged the development of an independent working-class political party?

The 30 years that followed the passing of the Third Reform Act saw profound changes in the economic and social structure of Britain. By 1914 Britain possessed a fully industrialised economy with a predominantly urban population. Also in this period, for the first time in the century, Britain's economic ascendancy was challenged, with Germany, France and the United States beginning to emerge as industrial powers in their own right. Although the British economy continued to grow, a price was clearly being paid for having been the first industrial nation. British firms were slow to innovate, and by 1900 it was difficult to escape the conclusion that British industry was failing to meet the challenge of what is often called the 'second industrial revolution'. As a result, most industries at this time registered a decline in profits.

Just as mid-Victorian confidence had been a reflection of Britain's role as the 'workshop of the world', so the emergence of serious economic competition seemed to replace the moral certainties of the earlier period with a sense of impending crisis. The period 1873 to 1896 is often called the 'Great Depression' in Britain. There has been considerable debate among historians over the appropriateness of this term, since this was not a depression in the accepted sense of a temporary decrease of production. Rather, it was a slowing of the rate of growth in the economy, particularly in comparison with the developing economies of Britain's trading rivals. By 1885 it had become apparent that economic growth was decelerating in Britain, and this served notice on people at the time that the mid-Victorian period of comparative economic and social stability was over.

This was largely because increased international competition meant that social relations within the workplace came under increasing stress. As firms struggled to maintain profit levels by raising productivity or by lowering wages, the industrial peace that had reached its zenith with the legalisation of trade unions in the 1870s gave way to a renewed social conflict that recalled the days of Chartism. In terms of working-class organisation, the period saw two major developments. First, there was an unprecedented growth of trade unionism. In 1880 only 5 per cent of the total workforce were members of trade unions, but by 1914 the figure had risen to 25 per cent. The most dramatic manifestations of this development were two major outbreaks of strikes in the years 1889–93 and 1910–14. Second, these years witnessed the emergence of a political party committed to the representation of working-class interests as its primary concern. In 1906 a group of 30 independent labour MPs were elected to Parliament and adopted as their name the 'Labour Party'. These two developments were closely linked as the new Labour Party drew strength from its role as the political arm of the growing trade union movement.

The emergence of an independent working-class political party in these years was a reflection of the social changes of the period – in particular, the opening up of the divisions between the classes. As we have seen, historians disagree on the extent to which a class society had existed in the first three-quarters of the nineteenth century. Yet, few historians would argue with the view that 'class' had become the most important determinant of social behaviour by the eve of the First World War. Many writers consider this to be the period that really saw the 'making' of the working class.

This process was partly geographical. The classes were more effectively segregated within the towns than ever before. New omnibus and tram services made possible the late nineteenth-century growth of genteel suburbs like Headingley (Leeds), Trafford (Manchester) and Edgbaston (Birmingham) to an extent previously undreamed of by the expanding lower middle class. The inner parts of the cities became the preserve of the working community, and a popular culture grew up based on the public house and the music hall. The fish and chip shop became a characteristic facility of these areas in the last quarter of the century, and by 1914 there were 25,000 of them in existence. The flat cloth-cap became standard dress for the working man. Seaside resorts like Blackpool, Scarborough, Bognor and Southend grew up to cater for the working-class day-tripper from the nearby towns. This period also saw the advent of Association Football as the 'people's game' and many of the clubs currently in existence can trace their origins to the late nineteenth century. When Tottenham Hotspur played Sheffield United in the FA Cup Final of 1901 the game attracted a crowd of 114,000. This cannot be entirely explained by the curiosity value of Billy Foulke, United's 21-stone goalkeeper and the largest man ever to play first-class football! Soccer had become part of a growing mass-based working-class culture, the existence of which eloquently testified to the separation of the classes in the years before 1914.

The economic changes of the period meant that this class division was accompanied by aggravated social problems. Ironically, in a period dubbed the 'Great Depression', the value of wages (the 'real wage'), was actually going up. Working people felt the benefit of international competition, particularly in the form of the cheaper foodstuffs now available from abroad as a result of the development of refrigerated transport. The rise in 'real wages' might have signalled a universal improvement in living standards were it not for the growth of the labour supply. The employable population grew by at least 10 per cent per decade between 1870 and 1910. Since this occurred during a slowing down of economic growth, it resulted in intense competition for jobs. Significantly, the word 'unemployed' appeared in the Oxford English Dictionary for the first time in 1882. This entry was extended for the 1888 edition to include the term 'unemployment', which had, by then, been recognised as one of the two major social problems of the day.

The other problem was housing. As the working class congregated in the city centres, forsaken for the suburbs by the middle class, the inability of the housing market to keep pace with population growth became apparent. In London, for example, the population had risen by 20 per cent per decade after 1860. All the evidence suggests that living conditions throughout Britain's cities were appalling. Even more alarming, these revelations cast doubt on the ability of the free market to deal with a problem on this scale. Yet a society based on a belief in individual enterprise as the key to economic and social advance was understandably reluctant to accept the need for extensive intervention by the state and local authorities to remedy the situation. Yet, even where there was sympathy with the 'poor', the understanding of the problems was limited by the dominant ideas of the day. In fact, the question debated by most reformers in the 1880s suggests that the idea of poverty as a self-inflicted wound was still popular. 'Is it the pig that makes the stye', the question went, 'or the stye that makes the pig?' A number of historians have pointed out that there was at least, by this time, a growing sense that, contrary to the 1834 orthodoxy, living conditions did affect social behaviour (and thus that the stye made the pig to some extent). Yet the important point about this debate, for anyone wanting to assess social attitudes of the period, is the language in which it was couched. The fact that working people were defined as 'pigs' by both sides of the argument is itself an indicator of the social separation that had taken place. The great fear, expressed by social reformers, was that, in the cities, an underclass or 'residuum' made up of the dregs of society was developing. There was much talk of a 'Pauper Frankenstein' that at some time might run amok.

The 'residuum' was seen as a growing threat, a 'dangerous class' that, by dragging the 'respectable' working class down into its vortex, might infect the whole of society. Edward Denison, the social reforming son of the Bishop of Salisbury, caught this mood of fear among members of his class with his rather extravagant description of a visit to Petticoat Lane market in the East End of London, in 1884; 'humanity swarms there in such quantity, of such quality, and in such streets, that I can only liken it to the trembling mass of maggots in a lump of carrion'. Both the severity of this imagery and its typicality makes it clear that the social problems of unemployment and living conditions were being discussed at a time of maximum distrust between the classes.

2 The Growth of Socialism

> **KEY ISSUE** What was the importance of socialist ideas and organisations, which emerged in the 1880s, for the development of an independent working-class political party?

From the 1880s onwards the belief that the free market could solve the problems it had created seemed increasingly ill-founded. Given this, it is perhaps not surprising that alternatives to *laissez-faire* liberalism began to appear. There emerged a body of socialist thought arguing that what was needed was a thoroughgoing change in the entire political and economic system. This growth of socialism was part of a Europe-wide phenomenon. The massacre of the Communards in Paris in 1871 had been widely deplored in Britain. Karl Marx's *Das Kapital* appeared in its first English translation in 1887. In the introduction to this English edition the author's friend Frederick Engels took more solace than most other commentators from the apparent disintegration of late Victorian society.

> 1 Each succeeding Winter brings up afresh the great question 'what to do with the unemployed'. But while the number of the unemployed keeps swelling from year to year there is nobody to answer that question and we can almost calculate the moment when the unemployed, losing
> 5 patience, will take their fate into their own hands.

In Britain the groundwork for a radical re-think of politics was laid by the American land reformer Henry George, whose book *Poverty and Progress* was published in 1879. Although he was not a socialist, George advocated a single tax on landownership to raise wages and improve conditions. Sales of his controversial book rose to 400,000 per year in 1882, and his view that the wealthy should be forced by the government to pay for better conditions for the poor gained a wide hearing.

The socialist thinkers who emerged in the 1880s went even further and advocated public ownership of the nation's assets. The year 1884 saw the establishment of three socialist organisations: the Social Democratic Federation, the Socialist League, and the Fabian Society. In their different ways each contributed to the public debate on social and political reform by arguing that there was an alternative to market capitalism. There were marked differences in the strategy adopted by these organisations, but each started from the assumption that a capitalist society was both unequal and exploitative in its nature.

The Social Democratic Federation (SDF) was formed by H.M. Hyndman. The son of a wealthy merchant, he enjoyed a private income which he augmented by speculating on the stock market. Hyndman had become a convert to Marxism in 1880 after reading *Das Kapital* on board a liner during a business trip to America. In the tradition of a long line of 'gentlemen reformers' he retained the trappings of his class, never forsaking the frock coat and top hat that became his trade marks at political meetings. Far from attempting to hide his social origins, Hyndman would pointedly thank working-class audiences for 'so generously supporting my class'. The SDF adopted what they called 'scientific socialism'. Following Marx closely, Hyndman advocated a policy of 'class warfare' leading to a revolution and a subsequent reorganisation of society along fairer lines. As the leading socialist organisation of the 1880s, the SDF drew a number of significant recruits into its ranks.

Among these was the poet and artist William Morris who swiftly broke with Hyndman to form the Socialist League. Like Hyndman, he came from a comfortable middle-class background and saw socialism as a way of reconstructing a divided society. Morris argued that industrialisation had separated the worker from the joy of creative work. In Marx's own terms this was the 'alienation' of the worker, the point at which workers simply became an extension of the machine on which they worked. Morris argued that industrialisation signalled the end of what we would call 'job satisfaction'. Because, to use his words, 'useful work' had become 'useless toil', the worker was distanced from the task being undertaken, employers became estranged from their employees and society became divided. Morris argued that society could be reconstructed as a 'Commonwealth', based on equality and a simple lifestyle. There was much in Morris's thinking that recalled the Owenites of the 1830s (see page 40), and certainly both have been condemned as being against mechanisation as such. In fact, both Owen and Morris were in favour of machinery. They simply wanted it to be used for the benefit of the workers who operated it, by abridging labour and improving living standards. However, Morris differed from the socialists of the 1830s in one respect. Like Hyndman, he accepted that it would require a revolution to bring about the desired changes. And in the spirit of Marx's writing he felt that capitalism contained the seeds of its own inevitable destruction. As he put it: 'the antagonism of classes, which the system has bred, is the natural and necessary instrument of its destruction'.

The third socialist organisation, formed in 1884, was the Fabian Society. This included in its ranks the Irish playwright George Bernard Shaw and a clerk from the Colonial Office called Sidney Webb. There is some debate among historians as to just how far the Fabians should now be seen as socialists at all. Unlike Hyndman and Morris (who followed Marx in this respect), they did not accept that a revolution was necessary before a society based on socialist principles could be established. They were firmly committed to reformism and advocated working for change slowly from within society's existing institutions, a strategy they referred to as 'permeation'. For the Fabians the problem of capitalism lay in its inefficiency. They thought that by working away to influence the government at both a local and national level it would be possible to construct efficient socialist institutions to work on behalf of the common good. Their first target for 'permeation' was the Liberal Party. In retrospect, this was rather a large objective for a group committed to gradualism. However much the Liberals (like the Conservatives) came to accept that reforms were needed, their commitment to the free market meant that they always remained some distance from a socialist approach. Such was Fabianism's concentration on the 'nuts and bolts' details of 'efficient' administration that it was often disparagingly referred to at the time as 'gas and water socialism'. Above all, the Fabians differed from other socialist organisations in that they did not see the militant working class as the historic agent of social and economic change. Since they felt, in the words of Sidney Webb, that change would have to be 'peaceful and constitutional', in its nature, they concentrated their efforts on the rational persuasion of those already in authority.

The importance of these socialist groups at this time should not be exaggerated. Their membership was small and each of the societies drew heavily on support from middle-class intellectuals, or 'drawing room socialists'. The Socialist League's paper, the *Commonweal*, edited by Morris, probably never had a circulation of more than 2,800. This compares rather badly with the *Northern Star* which sold 60,000 copies a week at the height of its popularity. Similarly, the SDF had a membership of only 1,000 in 1885 and when it put up two candidates in London constituencies in the election that year they polled a mere 59 votes between them. But both of these organisations can claim some success in orchestrating a London-based protest movement. The SDF, in particular, concentrated its efforts on the growing number of the unemployed in the capital. In 1886, during a particularly harsh winter, an SDF public open-air meeting of the unemployed turned into a riot, which *The Times* described as the greatest threat to private property since 1832. This was followed by two days of confrontations between demonstrators and police, greeted by Morris, ever the romantic, as 'the first skirmish of the Revolution'. In 1887 groups of the unemployed, organised by the SDF under the slogan 'Work not Charity', squatted in Trafalgar Square. On 13 November 1887 the

Square was cleared by baton-wielding police, in an incident in which 200 demonstrators were injured and which was immediately christened 'Bloody Sunday'.

The real importance of these socialist organisations lay in their propagation of alternative ideas at a time of social crisis. As we will see, these ideas, representing as they did a challenge to the orthodox free market thinking which continued to dominate the ideology of the Tories and the Liberals, formed the basis for the development of the Labour Party. These small socialist clubs also provided a political education for some of the most important union leaders of the period.

3 The Growth of Trade Unions: 'New Unionism for Old'

> **KEY ISSUES** Why did this period see a move away from the moderate trade unionism of the skilled workers in the mid-Victorian period towards strike action; what was new about 'new unionism'?

In the three years 1889–1891 the total membership of trade unions doubled. This 'explosion' of trade union activity was partly the result of the emergence of a number of new unions with a characteristically different approach to industrial relations. As we saw in the last chapter, the mid-Victorian 'model' unions, typified by the Amalgamated Society of Engineers, were exclusive bodies of skilled workers. Their high subscription rates restricted membership to the 'aristocracy of labour' and, because they represented such a small proportion of the workforce, they were to some extent accepted by employers.

The new unions of the 1880s were different in two important respects. First, they aimed at recruiting members among the less skilled sector of the workforce, many of whom had never previously been unionised. They were, therefore, less exclusive than the 'model' unions of the mid-Victorian period, and this was reflected in the fact that they levied lower subscriptions (generally in the region of a penny a week). Second, they tended to be more militant than their craft-based counterparts. This was only partly because they were, in the main, led by active socialists. The commitment of the new unions to strike action was really a reflection of the position occupied by their members in the workplace. Less skilled workers were more dispensable than skilled craftsmen. Employers were therefore less likely to make concessions to demands from their organisations. In short, any industrial action by the less skilled was likely to be confrontational.

The first clear sign that trade unions would never again be the preserve of the male elite of the labour force came in July 1888 when the women match workers at Bryant and May's factory in the East End of

London came out on strike against the horrific conditions in which they worked. They were encouraged in their action by Annie Besant, an influential middle-class socialist who was, rather unusually, a member of both the SDF and the Fabians. Besant, who was already well known as a campaigner for birth control, edited a socialist paper called *The Link*. In June 1888 in an article entitled 'White Slavery in London', she drew attention to the plight of one of the worst paid sectors of the workforce. Whilst Bryant and May paid shareholders a healthy dividend of 23 per cent, their women workers received an average of five shillings for a 70-hour week in some of the unhealthiest conditions industry had to offer. Nearly 1,400 women struck work for a fortnight in an action that brought significant concessions from the employers. Following the strike, a union was established among the workers at the factory, with 800 members by 1889 and Besant as Secretary.

The summer of 1889 saw two more victories for groups of workers organising themselves virtually for the first time. In March the Gas Workers and General Labourers' Union was formed in London by Will Thorne, a worker at the East Ham Gasworks. Thorne, an ex-navvy from Birmingham, was a member of the SDF and had been taught to read and write by Karl Marx's daughter, Eleanor. Within four months of its inception his union had 20,000 members throughout the country. In August 1889 Thorne brought his members out on strike demanding an eight-hour day. He was assisted in organising the strike by two other prominent members of the SDF, the engineering workers Tom Mann and John Burns. These three men epitomised the zeal of 'new unionism' and the way it was changing the face of trade unionism. John Burns was born into poverty in Lambeth as one of a family of ten children. A great believer in working-class political representation he had been elected, earlier in 1889, to the newly formed London County Council. Tom Mann started work in the mines of Warwickshire at the age of nine, having received less than three years' schooling. He established the Eight Hours League in 1886 to agitate for a reduction of hours across industry. This in itself marked a significant change in the direction of trade unionism, with an attempt to establish aims common to all industries. In a similar way, trade unionists began talking of the 'living wage', an issue that was of concern to all workers.

This attempt to address the general situation of all workers, rather than the sectional interests of one trade, was the key to the new unionism's style. 'Not since the high and palmy days of Chartism', noted the old Chartist leader George Julian Harney in 1889, 'have I witnessed a movement corresponding in importance and interest.' This comparison with Chartism is important for an understanding of the impact of new unionism. Mass support was being mobilised once more, utilising strategies from the Chartist tradition. John Burns, for example, was a platform orator with a style of delivery of which O'Connor might have been proud, but with one important difference. Burns was not a 'gentleman reformer'. Born into poverty, he addressed working-class audiences on the issues of the day from personal experience.

Thorne's union was successful in its strike and this acted as an inspiration to other groups of workers. Burns, Thorne and Mann now turned their attention to London's docks. A small dispute had broken out at the South West India Dock over the method of piecework payment. The men were led by Ben Tillett, an ex-sailor who was now a tea porter. The dispute swiftly escalated. The dockers were employed on an entirely casual basis; they had to apply for work each day at the dock gates. Their work was punishing and their pay was abysmally low. Tillett, assisted by Burns, Mann and Thorne, now set about drawing all the 'dock rats', as they were scornfully called, into the dispute. They framed a demand for a minimum wage of sixpence an hour, the 'docker's tanner', and persuaded the Stevedores' Union, which represented the skilled dock workers, to come out in support.

As casual workers, the dockers were very vulnerable to replacement by other workers. But the strike was solid. With 150,000 men on strike, for a month almost nothing was shipped through the Port of London, the heart of the nation's trade. Each day Burns led a huge procession through the City. The orderly nature of these demonstrations won the widespread support of public opinion, which had feared a repeat of the riots of 1887. The strike was hugely expensive for the union. At one point the meagre strike pay it was able to give its members still totalled £1,250 per day. But the dockers were supported financially by workers both at home and abroad. Australian trade unionists contributed £30,000. The British public seemed to rally to the dock workers as the downtrodden group conducting themselves with quiet dignity. Even the Stock Exchange made a contribution to strike funds! Eventually, an unlikely arbitrator between employers and employees appeared in the shape of Cardinal Manning, the Roman Catholic Archbishop of Westminster. His intercession in this role was acceptable to the dockers since many of them were Irish Catholics. The strike ended, in an almost carnival atmosphere, with victory for the dockers.

Following the strike, the small tea operatives' union that Tillett had formed in 1886 was re-modelled as the Dock, Wharf, Riverside and General Labourers' Union. Tom Mann became the union's first President, and it had 56,000 members by 1890. Undoubtedly, this was the most lasting effect of the dock strike. Tillett's union was to remain in existence until 1920, when it was again re-modelled, this time as the Transport and General Workers' Union. The age of mass general unionism seemed to have arrived. A seamen's union, established in 1889, for example, had a membership of 65,000 by 1891. In a similar way, the General Railway Workers' Union, formed in 1889, aimed at drawing in the unskilled grades of worker excluded by the more 'aristocratic' Amalgamated Society of Railway Servants, which had been established in 1871.

These 'new unionists' attended the TUC for the first time in 1890. Their impact may be seen in the fact that in that year, not only did the Congress agree to back the demand for an eight-hour day, it also gave its name and support to the first May Day celebrations ever to have been held in Britain. This reflected changes in some of the older craft unions. The relationship established between the skilled unions and the employers by 1875 was now deteriorating. In the conditions of intensified international competition that had become apparent by the late 1880s, employers could no longer afford to respect the demarcation of skills as defined by the craft unions.

Under pressure to compete more effectively, employers looked at ways of 'rationalising' their firms by increasing productivity. Machinery became faster and the demands on the worker became correspondingly greater. In order to give added incentives to work hard, in many industries weekly wages were replaced by piecework. Employers became more aware of the way workers used their time in the workplace. Working in a railway engineering works in Swindon before the First World War, one worker complained of a supervisor who 'is in the habit of standing over the boys at the lathe, watch in hand, for four hours without once moving, and, by his manner and language, compelling them to run at an excessive rate so as to cut their prices.' After 1910 this kind of approach was popularised as 'scientific management', but its impact had been felt long before that date in British industry, particularly in the heavy engineering trades. These trades, from which had once emerged 'new model' unionists like William Allen, now produced more radical leaders like Burns and Mann. Confronted with this new situation even the older unions recognised that they needed to re-organise themselves to meet the challenge.

Certainly, most unions took advantage of the temporary improvement in trade, and the consequent demand for labour, between 1889 and 1891, to expand membership and to re-organise their structure. The mineworkers, for example, had a long history of industrial organisation, having established local associations in most areas in the 1860s. In 1889, following a series of successful wage demands throughout the pit areas, the Miners' Federation of Great Britain was established. This included most of the local associations, and it supported the call of the 'new' unions for an eight-hour day. Most of the older unions, established in the mid-Victorian period, increased their membership in the last two decades of the nineteenth century, to such an extent that by 1900 the 'new' unionists accounted for less than one third of all trade unionists. Many of the older unions, recognising that the main threat to them lay in the use of less skilled workers to do their jobs, opened their ranks to lower grades of workers. The Amalgamated Society of Railway Servants, denied official recognition by the railway companies, dropped their prohibition on the entry of less skilled railway workers. The cotton textile workers of Lancashire began to open their unions to women, although in this respect they were still unusual.

Overall, the period from 1889 to 1891 was of great significance for the future of organised labour. The clear determination of unions to recruit more widely than previously mirrored an increasingly antagonistic relationship between labour and capital in British industry. However, many of the specific gains of these years were shortlived. As the temporary trade boom collapsed and the spectre of unemployment returned at the end of 1891, the employers struck back.

4 The Employers' Response: Free Labour, Collective Bargaining and Legal Action

> **KEY ISSUE** How successfully did the employers respond to 'new unionism' in the 1890s?

If the logic of the changing social and economic situation in the late nineteenth century suggested the need for greater organisation and solidarity among the workforce, the same was also increasingly true for the employers. Their commitment to economic competition with rival firms rather than co-operation, obviously militated against the creation of employers' organisations. However, faced with the burgeoning of trade unions in the 1880s, and the need to meet the threat from abroad by introducing radical changes in the workplace, employers drew together to defend their common interests. They did this by forming associations for mutual support and also by utilising the law. Whenever they took unions on in the 1890s they invariably won. The legacy of bitterness that this counterattack engendered was to be long lasting. Most importantly, it was to ensure trade union support for the establishment of the Labour Party in the early years of the twentieth century.

The Shipping Federation was formed in 1890 and set to work to break the hold of the dockside and seamen's unions in the ports. It included in its ranks the owners of nearly 90 per cent of British merchant vessels, and in November 1890 it refused to recognise the settlement that had ended the Dock strike of the previous year. With the use of non-union labour, it effectively drove Tillett's union from the London docks. Over the next three years there were strikes against the Federation at most British ports, culminating in a major defeat for the union at Hull in 1893. Here, the army and naval gunboats were used to protect strike-breakers. The impact of the employers' victory can be seen in the decline of dock-union membership. In 1890 Tillett's union claimed some 56,000 members. By the end of 1892 this had fallen to 23,000 and, by 1900, to just under 14,000.

From 1893 onwards, employers wishing to replace striking workers with a non-union workforce could use the facilities offered by William Collison's National Free Labour Association. Collison, a Londoner, had served in the army before helping to organise a union of busmen in the capital. Turning to strike-breaking, he registered somewhere in the region of 850,000 workmen as 'free-labourers' between 1893 and 1913. Collison's Association was financed by employers and his 'black-legs' were invariably protected by the police or the army. Nevertheless, using his services was not without its difficulties. As one employer put it: 'the men that Collison sent me were mere labourers, and the worst band of ruffians and scoundrels you can imagine. I was delighted to be rid of them.'

The employers hit back in the 1890s in two other major industries: cotton textiles and mining. In Lancashire the employers formed the Federation of Master Cotton Spinners in 1891 and cut wages by 5 per cent in the following year. The ensuing lock-out of workers refusing to agree to the cuts lasted into early 1893. It was eventually resolved with the Brooklands Agreement which established the machinery of collective bargaining for the industry. A joint committee of employers and union representatives would in future determine wage levels in relation to the price of cotton. In the mining areas employers responded in a similar way. A fall in the price of coal led the owners in the Yorkshire, Lancashire and Midlands coalfields to demand a 25 per cent reduction in wage levels. The newly formed miners' union (the Miners' Federation of Great Britain) found itself confronted with an unprecedented unity of action on the part of the owners. From July 1893 every pit in these areas locked out its workforce to force it to agree to the new terms. The dispute lasted until November, involving 300,000 miners and a series of clashes between troops and strikers which left two miners dead at a colliery near Featherstone in Yorkshire. It was finally ended by government intervention: Prime Minister Gladstone ordered the Foreign Secretary, Lord Rosebery, to bring the two sides together for a settlement. As a result a Conciliation Board was established, but the miners' demand for a minimum wage was not conceded.

This was the first strike to have been settled through the intervention of the government, and for many this, as well as the Brooklands Agreement in the cotton industry, seemed to point the way forward. Because of the scale of organisation on both sides, strikes and lock-outs had come to have a crippling effect on the economy. The Conciliation Act of 1896 gave the Board of Trade the power to appoint conciliators to settle disputes. But this was to be a voluntary process and the Board would only act if its help was requested by one of the parties. There was no attempt to impose compulsory arbitration on parties in dispute. The Act did much to further the argument for disputes to be settled by the intervention of third parties, but it lacked the authority of legal compulsion and put its faith in the goodwill of the two sides involved. The great engineering lock-out of the following year suggested that this faith was misplaced.

The tensions in the engineering industry, caused by the introduction of new methods of work, came to a head in 1897. The Engineering Employers' Federation had been formed in 1896, with the avowed intent of reducing the control over production exercised by the Amalgamated Society of Engineers. When the ASE demanded an eight-hour day in July 1897 it found itself locked out by nationwide action taken by the employers. The dispute lasted until January 1898 and ended in a humiliating defeat for the union. The employers imposed a settlement on the ASE which established that the union would not 'interfere' with 'the management of business'. Collective bargaining clauses in the agreement ensured against 'unofficial' strikes by local branches, by insisting that all decisions to cease work be approved by the ASE executive.

Thus, in the major industries the employers came together to meet the threat of the new spirit of militancy in the unions. This was consolidated by the establishment of the Employers' Federation's Parliamentary Committee in 1898 to lobby Parliament in the same way as the TUC's Parliamentary Committee. Historians have sometimes argued that by consolidating their own organisations the employers were clearly bent on the destruction of the trade unions. This is too simple a view of what was happening. In fact, the settlement of the disputes in coal, cotton and engineering gives a good insight into the aims of employers at this time. It was not that they wanted, in the main, to destroy trade unions as organisations. After all, it had been demonstrated earlier in the century that compliant unions, who were prepared to discipline their members, were useful to employers. It was in the employers' interests to have strong centralised unions with an acknowledged, but restricted, role in the workplace. Thus, most of these disputes, where unions were defeated, resulted not in the eradication of the unions but rather in the establishment of collective bargaining procedures for those industries. These procedures actually reaffirmed the existence of the unions as organisations but ensured that future disputes would be settled in a way that was favourable to the employers. In this way, the employers' counter-attack created divisions within the unions between those officials who wished to continue with the militancy that had been re-born with 'new unionism', and those who felt that there was more to be gained by working within the constraints of collective bargaining, even if this was on the employers' terms. Sometimes the distinction was between a cautious union executive at head office, and the militant 'rank and file' in the localities. Employers did all they could to limit the power of the militants within the unions, as a way of producing the kind of moderate trade unionism with which they were most comfortable.

The main source of power for militant trade unionism was, as always, the strike reinforced by well organised picketing. Such activity had been given legal status by the legislation of the 1870s. In the

1890s, however, employers began to contest this legality by a series of court actions. In three cases in the 1890s employers attempted successfully to restrict the actions a union could take in picketing during an industrial dispute. This effort was consolidated in 1901 by the notorious Taff Vale decision.

Following a strike in August 1900 by members of the Amalgamated Society of Railway Servants against the Taff Vale Railway Company in South Wales, the Company sued the union for damages caused to their business. The court upheld the Company's case, and although this was quashed on appeal, the House of Lords found in favour of the original decision in 1901. Damages in this case were set at £23,000 and the union was ordered to pay. This had enormous implications for all trade unions since it meant that they were considered in law to be corporate bodies which could be sued for actions committed on their behalf by their officials. In the case of Quinn v Leathem, heard by the Lords two weeks after their decision on Taff Vale, it was held that the threat of industrial action could be considered a conspiracy to injure. Given the earlier Taff Vale decision, a union could be sued for damages in such a case in its corporate capacity.

After Taff Vale a union could be sued for damages for organising a strike; after Quinn v Leathem it could be sued for planning a strike. All the achievements of the 1860s and the 1870s in establishing legal status for the unions had been reversed. The unions had re-entered the semi-legal position they had occupied in the wake of the repeal of the Combination Acts in 1824; they were legal bodies but when they acted they were likely to break the law. Yet there were mixed reactions to Taff Vale within the unions. A few cautious union leaders hoped that, by discouraging strikes, the decision would help them discipline their militant 'rank and file'.

But most trade unionists do seem to have been alarmed at the implications of the Taff Vale decision. It demonstrated the vulnerability of the unions and the need for legislation that would verify their right to use industrial action on behalf of their members. Neither the Liberals nor the Conservatives were keen to introduce such a measure. Both political parties tended to side with the employers when it came to industrial action. Since the late 1880s there had been socialist groups arguing that working people needed their own parliamentary party. Hitherto, the unions had not been persuaded of this need. Their position seemed secure and politically they could operate by lobbying the existing parties. Taff Vale changed this and the unions suddenly saw the potential benefits of independent labour representation. Their support was to be decisive in the emergence of the Labour Party.

5 The Evolution of the Labour Party

> **KEY ISSUES** Why did it take so long for an independent working-class political party to appear? How were its form and its policies influenced by Liberalism and its links with the trade unions?

a) From Lib-Lab to Labour

Looking at the creation of the Labour Representation Committee (LRC) in 1900 and the Labour Party in 1906, what seems to require explanation is not so much why it came about but rather why it took so long in coming. There had been an articulate radical working-class presence in British politics, in one form or another, since 1815. Manhood suffrage, as introduced by 1884, was undoubtedly crippled by the cumbersome registration qualifications with which it had been deliberately hedged. But even when account is taken of this, little of substance seems to have been achieved in terms of getting working-class representatives into Parliament by the end of the century. The Chartists would surely have shaken Westminster to its foundations had the 1884 franchise been available in 1839. As it was, the working-class voters chose either Liberals or Conservatives to represent their interests. And although the Liberals were the main beneficiaries of working-class support, working-class Conservatism was strong in Lancashire, often as a form of opposition to Liberal employers.

Working-class support for the parties of Land and Commerce can best be seen as a manifestation of the mid-Victorian social compact between the 'respectable' working class and their 'betters'. In return for important political concessions from both parties (the vote, legalisation of trade unions, and limited social reform), working-class activists forsook the boisterous radicalism of Chartism for the shared values of a society emphasising self-help and respectability. But by the end of the nineteenth century it was becoming clear that neither popular Liberalism nor popular Conservatism could really 'deliver the goods'. The Liberal Party accepted working men as parliamentary candidates in some areas. But there were a mere eight 'Lib-Lab' MPs in 1889, and this number had only increased to 11 by 1900. Around half of these were from coal-mining areas where the closeness of the community and a well-developed trade union tradition made it relatively easy to raise the funds to support working men in the unpaid role of MP. The idea of Lib-Lab representatives had seemed promising in the 1870s, but the result was a sparse and geographically very patchy representation of the working community. Even when the Lib-Lab MP Henry Broadhurst, an ex-stonemason and the Secretary of the TUC, became the first working man to achieve government office when he was made Under Secretary at the Home Office in Gladstone's government of 1886, it seemed a token gesture. It was difficult to escape the conclusion that this was a very one-sided relationship between a middle-class leadership and a working-class 'rank and file'. Also, neither party's attempts at social reform seemed to address the issues of importance to the working class, particularly unemployment, the eight-hour day and housing. The Liberals suffered a significant defeat in the election of 1895 and seemed to be absorbed with the issue of Irish Home rule.

The working-class support for the Liberal Party that had so appalled Marx and Engels in 1868 and that had been such a feature of political life in the 1870s, was now being questioned by a number of working-class activists. It was the expansion of trade unions that caused this change. The new, and militant, trade unionism of the 1880s and the 1890s re-opened the debate on the distribution of wealth that had been pushed into the background since the demise of Chartism. It was difficult for the classes to stress their common values within a political alliance whilst confronting the issue that divided them most: the relationship between wages and profit. This shift, from Liberalism to a commitment to independent working-class representation, can perhaps best be seen in the personal development of James Keir Hardie.

Hardie was born the illegitimate son of a farm-servant, Mary Keir, in Lanarkshire, Scotland in 1856. As a child he worked in the coal-pits near Hamilton. His education was extremely rudimentary. His mother taught him to read using scraps of newspaper she picked up in the street. He taught himself to write using a pin to scratch a stone blackened with the smoke of his pit lamp. As an adult he became a skilled face-worker and a leading trade unionist among the Ayrshire miners. He was also a Nonconformist, a teetotaller and a Liberal, working hard to persuade the miners to vote Liberal when they were enfranchised in 1884. In 1886 he visited London and met members of the SDF. In drafting the rules of the Ayrshire miners later the same year, he seems to have already shifted away from a Liberal standpoint. The introduction of the rules states: 'All wealth is created by Labour. . . . Capital, which is created by labour, had become the master of its creator.' He finally became disenchanted with the Liberal Party and convinced of the need for independent labour representation, as a result two events: the breaking of a strike among the Lanarkshire miners in 1887 where police and the army had used a good deal of violence, and the failure of the Liberal opposition in Parliament to support the Scottish miners' call for an eight-hour day to be established by legislation.

Hardie was nominated as an independent candidate, sponsored by the miners, in the Mid-Lanarkshire by-election of 1888. This was the first time an independent Labour candidate had stood against the two main parties. Although he was defeated, he took heart from the 614 votes he received and two weeks after the by-election he established the Scottish Labour Party. This was the first time the term 'Labour

Party' had been used in British politics. The party remained small with just 23 branches established by 1893. But it managed to field five candidates, albeit unsuccessfully, in the general election of 1892. Hardie was becoming known outside Scotland, particularly for his attacks on the Lib-Lab members at the TUC. London radicals and socialists, including Will Thorne, persuaded him to stand as an independent Labour candidate for West Ham South in the general election of 1892. He was elected, as were two other independent Labour candidates, John Burns for Battersea, and the leader of the seamen's union, Joseph Havelock Wilson, for Middlesborough. Hardie's supporters in West Ham, largely new unionists from the East End, sent him to Parliament in a two-horse charabanc with a trumpeter to announce his progress. The Lib-Lab MPs had always been careful to appear in the House 'properly' dressed in top hat and tails, but Hardie wore his ordinary clothes, a deerstalker hat and a tweed suit with a check so loud that John Burns claimed he could have played draughts on it. Hardie was simply making the point – that he was to stick to throughout his political career – that independent Labour MPs should retain their independence inside the House of Commons. There was much of this feeling in his references to himself as 'the member for the unemployed'.

b) The Independent Labour Party

The movement towards an independent representation for the working class was also gaining ground in the north of England. In Lancashire Joe Burgess, a textile worker turned journalist, propounded the idea in his newspaper, the *Workman's Times*. The same message was given out by Robert Blatchford in his enormously successful paper, the *Clarion*. In 1891 Blatchford, sacked from a lucrative job on the *Sunday Chronicle* because of his socialist views, helped to form the Manchester Labour Party, modelled on Hardie's Scottish example. Over the next two years Labour Unions were formed in Bradford, Colne Valley, Huddersfield, Halifax and Keighley. In the words of the Bradford Labour Union, the aim of these associations was to 'further the cause of direct Labour representation on local bodies and in Parliament'. In 1893 Hardie was asked to chair a conference in Bradford to bring these labour organisations together and unite them with those in other areas. From this meeting the Independent Labour Party (ILP) was born.

Among the 120 delegates who met in Bradford there were few from areas already represented by Lib-Lab MPs, like the mining areas of Northumberland and Durham, and the Midlands. The Fabians and the SDF sent delegates, but the London socialist groups thought little could come of the move. More than a third of the delegates came from Yorkshire, and most of them from O'Connor's old stronghold, the West Riding. This area, and particularly Bradford, had by this time become the focus of the demand for Labour representation. On the face of it, this was an unlikely location. It was dominated politically by families of large Liberal Nonconformist employers, supported by working men's Liberal Associations. In the 1880s working men had begun to contest seats on local councils with some success. Yet when William Morris lectured in Bradford in 1884 he found his working-class audience rather unresponsive to his message. He concluded that they were a 'sad set of Philistines'. However, less than a decade later, Bradford was leading the call for independent labour representation. In Bradford, as in so many other places, it was the experience of industrial conflict that had been the catalyst for change. The attempt by the owners of Manningham Mills, a large local woollen firm, to lower their employees' wages by 15–30 per cent in 1890 led to a pro-tracted, and often violent, strike involving the Weavers' Association and thousands of workers. Although the owners, backed by the other textile employers in the area, were able to break the strike in 1891, the general harmony of relations between the classes had been irrevocably destroyed in the process. As the textile workers' newspaper, the *Yorkshire Factory Times,* put it: 'Labour has so associated itself that even defeat must be victory'. The creation of the Independent Labour Party, at a conference held at the Bradford Labour Union two years later, seemed to confirm this prophecy.

The ILP was a national organisation with a socialist programme. It committed itself to 'secure the collective ownership of the means of production, distribution and exchange'. It therefore argued that, in its vision of the future, 'the people', rather than individuals, would control and run the economy. But this was a version of socialism that was identifiably British in its nature. It drew on the three important traditional roots – of liberalism, trade unionism, and Nonconformity – and this made it very different from its more revolutionary socialist counterparts on the Continent. Hardie, for example, led the Conference in its rejection of the 'class war' strategies of the SDF. Many of the ILP's leading lights in its early years were recent converts from the Liberal Party. James Ramsay MacDonald, a warehouse clerk turned journalist, had spent four years as a private secretary to a radical Liberal MP. In 1894, disillusioned by the unwillingness of the Liberals to accept working men as parliamentary candidates, he made the break and joined the ILP. He would, of course, go on to become the first Labour Prime Minister, but his route from 'Liberalism' to 'Labourism' was typical of many who came to support independent labour representation. Inevitably, this influenced the nature of the new party. The programme and approach of the ILP bore the hallmarks of its progenitors' earlier commitment to liberalism. There was, for example, a total acceptance that the parliamentary, rather than the revolutionary, path was the correct one to take. Progress would be made by persuasion and change would come gradually by a process of reforming existing institutions rather than by overthrowing them.

Along with a background in the Liberal Party, many of the ILP's supporters came to the new party through the experience of trade unionism and this could be seen in the pragmatism of its programme. Whilst this spoke of the need for an 'Industrial Commonwealth founded upon the Socialisation of Land and Commerce', it was less specific on how this should be achieved. The ILP was always more comfortable with specific and concrete aims, like the call for Old Age Pensions and the eight-hour day, than with developing theories of class struggle. John Burns referred to the theory of socialism as 'the chattering of Continental magpies'. Within the ILP, Hardie always played up this pragmatic approach. He felt that to broaden its appeal to trade unionists weaned on the approach of the Liberal Party, the ILP needed to stress its moderation. He even insisted that the term 'socialist' should not appear in the name of the party, arguing 'labour' was of broader appeal.

The third major tradition from which the ILP drew its version of socialism was Nonconformist religion. In leaders such as Hardie and Phillip Snowden, a young clerk from the West Riding, the importance of Nonconformity was clearly evident. These were men who were more familiar with the Bible than with Marx. As Hardie was fond of explaining: 'The final goal of Socialism, is a form of Social Economy very closely akin to the principles set forth in the Sermon on the Mount.' Like Hardie, Snowden's socialism was never doctrinaire but his emotional platform style, known to his supporters as 'Phillip's come to Jesus', was a reminder of earlier days when the North had resounded to the oratory of the Chartist leader the Revd J.R. Stephens. This was a version of socialism that drew heavily on emotive imagery and religious justification. One historian, examining those areas of the North and Scotland where the ILP expanded rapidly over the next few years, has referred to this phenomenon as the 'religion of socialism'. The enthusiasm generated in some areas certainly seems to have taken on aspects of a religious revival in terms of its energy and zest.

The British version of socialism that lay behind the demand for labour representation was direct, uncomplicated, pragmatic and morally forthright. A good example of this approach can be seen in Robert Blatchford's newspaper, the *Clarion*. Blatchford became a leading member of the ILP, and his paper, published in Manchester, achieved a regular circulation of 35,000. Readers were encouraged to form social groups for discussion and mutual support and, in particular, the Clarion Cycling Clubs became enormously popular. Through 1892 and 1893 Blatchford wrote a series of letters for the paper addressed to 'John Smith of Oldham', in which he explained the nature of socialism. A cheap collected version of these articles was published in 1894 as the book *Merrie England,* and this sold a phenomenal one million copies over the next few years. Here, British workers were presented with an interpretation of socialism that was reassuringly accessible:

1 Socialism, John, does not consist in violently seizing upon the property
of the rich and sharing it out among the poor. ... Practical Socialism is
so simple that a child may understand it. It is a kind of national scheme
of co-operation managed by the State. Its programme consists, essen-
5 tially of one demand, that the land and other instruments of production
shall be the common property of the people, and shall be used and governed by the people for the people. ... Socialists point out that if all the
industries of the nation were put under State control, all the profit that
now goes into the hands of a few idle men, would go into the coffers of
10 the State – which means that the people would enjoy the benefits of all
the wealth they create. ... But Practical Socialism would do more than
that. It would educate the people. It would provide cheap and pure
food. It would extend and elevate the means of study and amusement.
... What are the things to be done? We want to find work for the
15 unemployed. We want to get pensions for the aged. We want to abolish the poor law system. We want to produce our own food so as to
be independent of foreign nations. We want to get rid of the slums and
build good houses for the workers. We want to abolish the sweater
and shorten hours of labour and raise wages. We want to get rid of the
20 smoke nuisance, and the pollution of the rivers; and we want to place
the land and all other instruments of production under the control of
the State. But before we can accomplish any of these reforms we must
have a public in favour of them, and a Parliament that will give effect to
the Popular demands.

Despite the impact of the 'religion of socialism' in some areas, and
the adhesion of 35,000 paid up members by 1895, the ILP met with a
good deal of working-class opposition, particularly from the trade
unions. Worried that the formation of the ILP would eventually lead
to the domination of the TUC by socialists from the new unions, the
TUC's Parliamentary Committee introduced the 'block vote' in 1895.
Previously, each delegate's vote counted equally, now they would be
counted in proportion to the number of members in the union represented by the delegate. This served to strengthen the hand of the
older unions, with their greater commitment to working with the
existing political parties and developing the machinery of collective
bargaining. As one Lib-Lab union leader put it: 'We saw that congress
was losing whatever influence it had, and we were determined to pull
it back again into the old paths.' At the same time the TUC voted to
exclude delegates from the Trades' Councils, which had, in many
areas, been taken over by ILP supporters.

A further setback was suffered by the ILP when all 28 of its candidates, including Hardie, were defeated in the general election of
1895. The party also found itself isolated with the outbreak of war
against the Boers in South Africa in 1899. The ILP's anti-war stance
ran counter to the jingoism engendered for what was widely expected
to be a short and successful war against weak opponents. The ILP was

labelled 'pro-Boer' and became the object of popular hostility. In these years it became clear to Hardie, and to others within the party, that encouraging enthusiastic support at the 'grass roots' was an unpredictable process. His objective became a 'Labour alliance' of all those disparate groups who wanted to increase the parliamentary representation of working people. This was a reluctant recognition that most working-class organisations were not socialist and that, therefore, the ILP would never vie with the major parties for power unless it subsumed its socialism within an alliance of wider working-class political opinion.

The opportunity to launch such an alliance came from the TUC conference of 1899. The Amalgamated Society of Railway Servants introduced a resolution calling on the Parliamentary Committee to convene a conference of all organisations committed to 'securing a better representation of the interests of labour in the House of Commons'. The resolution was passed by 546,000 votes to 434,000, an indication of the extent to which trade unionists were divided over the advisability of independent labour representation. Most of the votes against were exercised by the coal and cotton unions. Yet their satisfaction with the status quo was no longer typical. Trade unions generally were reeling under the concerted counter-attack of employers, and parliamentary representation was seen as a means of self defence.

c) The Labour Representation Committee

The 129 delegates who met in February 1900, in response to the TUC's resolution, came from the socialist societies (the SDF, Fabians and the ILP), and 67 trade unions representing about a quarter of total trade union membership at the time. The conference was a resounding success for the ILP. It was able to steer the delegates between the 'class war' advocated by the SDF, and the desire of some of the trade unionists to limit the parliamentary actions of working-class MPs to particular issues. Hardie's resolution to create an organisation that would support a 'distinct Labour group in Parliament who shall have their own whips and agree upon their own policy' was accepted. He would have liked this to be called the 'United Labour Party' but the conference opted for the title 'Labour Representation Committee' as being less contentious. With ILP man Ramsay MacDonald as Secretary, the Committee consisted of two ILP members, two SDF members, one Fabian and seven trade unionists.

This marked the birth of the Labour Party in all but name. There are a number of characteristics that may be identified in its origins that determined the sort of party it would be in the future. It had emerged from a trade union initiative; trade union support would always be important in the future. It contained within it socialist organisations of various kinds, but its manifesto was not overtly socialist. A new word, 'socialistic', had crept into the debate, meaning generally sympathetic to the broad aims of socialism, but without a firm adhesion to state ownership. The LRC was 'socialistic' and Hardie was prepared to accept this compromise as the price of union support. This was too much for the SDF who rapidly disaffiliated. Many of the activists had close links with the Liberal Party, and the LRC was open to any political alliance that would assist the election of their candidates, without compromising their independence. Thus the LRC was drawn from groups with rather different objectives, who were aware of the political realities of the day and were prepared to sink their differences to achieve a common goal. So whatever linked the men involved in this endeavour, there were inherent tensions built into the structure of the LRC, especially between socialists and moderate trade unionists, and these would not go away in the years to come.

Nevertheless, the new organisation got off to a good start when two of its candidates, Keir Hardie and Richard Bell, were elected for Merthyr and Derby respectively in the general election of 1900. Bell, who was the Secretary of the Amalgamated Society of Railway Servants, was no socialist. But the ASRS had been consistently refused recognition by the railway companies, and it saw parliamentary action as the way to secure a legal status for all unions. This point was made emphatically by the drama that unfolded at Taff Vale later that same year, and which involved Bell's union. The Lords' judgement on the case in 1901 had the effect of converting previously sceptical unions to the cause of independent labour representation, and it was this that really launched the LRC as a political force.

Both Liberal and Conservative parties baulked at introducing legislation to protect the unions following Taff Vale, but the LRC was now on hand as the logical political alternative to which the unions could turn. As a result of the Lords' ruling, 127 unions joined the LRC, including the Engineers and the Textile Workers, raising total membership from 353,000 before the ruling to 847,000 by 1903. Additional union affiliations followed over the next few years (though the Miners' Federation did not join until 1909) and affiliating unions levied their members to provide financial support for the LRC. The crucial link, sought by Hardie, between the parliamentary representation of working people and their most important organisations, the trade unions, had been secured as a result of the employers' campaign against the unions, culminating in Taff Vale. In 1904 Ramsay MacDonald explained in a speech to the TUC that: 'The Labour Representation Committee is neither sister nor brother to the Congress, but its child'.

Summary Diagram

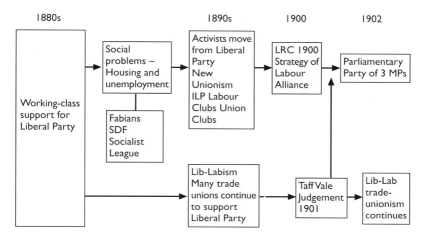

| 1880s | | 1890s | 1900 | 1902 |

The key to understanding the Labour Party as a political force lies in appreciating the nature of its origins. It emerged from liberalism and moderate trade unionism at a time when both were being recognised as inadequate to meet the social problems of the day. Its leaders adopted a very particular form of socialism, that was reformist rather than revolutionary, and you need to capture the special quality of this in your notetaking. Above all, the Labour Party emerged as the political arm of the trade unions and this always influenced both its strength and its policies. You should be careful in your notetaking not to separate the history of these two organisations. Your notes on the period 1885–1902 could be organised under the following headings:

1 Economic and social developments that divided the classes
2 Developments in trade unionism that made an independent political party attractive
3 Origins of reformism – links with Liberalism.

A section on answering structured and essay questions on this period appears as part of the next chapter.

1. Robert Blatchford, *Merrie England*

Read the extract from Blatchford's book on page 120. Answer the following questions:

a) Why did Blatchford address his book to 'John Smith'? (*2 marks*)
b) What does he mean by 'Practical Socialism' and how might this be different to any other sort of Socialism? (*4 marks*)
c) What does he want to achieve? (*4 marks*)
d) How does he intend to achieve it? (*4 marks*)
e) Identify as many ways as you can in which this approach to social reform is different from that depicted by the documents studied in section 1 above. (*6 marks*)
f) Why might the approach taken in the passage appeal to working people?

6 Labour in Parliament 1902–14

POINTS TO CONSIDER

From the vantage of hindsight it sometimes seems obvious that an independent party would at some stage emerge to represent the working-class voter. The collapse of the Liberal Party in the 1920s and 1930s seems to confirm the inevitability of this development. However, this was not how it looked in the period leading up to the First World War. Most working-class voters were happy within the Liberal Party and, since most of the leaders of the Labour Party had originally been Liberals, it was often hard for the new party to establish itself as offering something distinctive. This was particularly so when the Liberals took on a social reform agenda after their landslide electoral victory in 1906. To compound the problem, the growth of militant trade unionism, in the form of syndicalism, offered the strategy of direct action to working people in place of the 'reformism' of Labour leaders like Hardie and MacDonald. To understand the actions of the Labour Party in Parliament it is necessary for us to think back into the period prior to 1918 when Labour's hold on the working-class voter appeared to be threatened by a range of factors.

KEY DATES

1903 Arthur Henderson, leader of the Ironworkers, wins by-election in Barnard Castle.

1903 Ramsay MacDonald negotiates electoral agreement with Liberals; Emmeline Pankhurst forms Women's Social and Political Union.

1905 George Sorel publishes *Reflections on Violence*, the founding text of Syndicalism.

1906 Liberal landslide victory at general election; 29 Labour Representation Committee candidates elected, they assume the name Labour Party; Trade Disputes Act passed.

1908 Liberals introduce Old Age Pensions; Ben Tillett publishes *Is the Parliamentary Labour Party a Failure?*; the ILP publish *Let Us Reform the Labour Party*.

1909 Miners' Federation affiliate to the Labour Party; Osborne judgement rules it is illegal for unions to compel payment of political levy by members.

1910 January general election, 40 of the 70 Labour candidates elected; in the December election 42 are successful; coal strike in South Wales.

1911 One miner shot dead, and others injured, by troops in Tonypandy; salaries introduced for MPs.

1912 Labour launches its own newspaper *The Daily Citizen*; George Lansbury launches *The Daily Herald*; (February to April) first ever national coal strike; strikes among dockers and transport workers; over one million workers strike during this year in a total of 857 strikes.

1913 A total of 1497 strikes recorded nationally involving over 500, 000 workers.

1914 Triple Alliance agreement signed by miners, railway workers and transport workers.

1918 Representation of the People Act.

1 Labour and the Liberals

> **KEY ISSUE** How could the new Labour Party demonstrate in Parliament and in the country that it had something distinctive to offer the working-class voter?

In most constituencies where the Labour Representation Committee hoped to be successful, their main rivals for the working-class vote were the Liberals. Having been defeated in the general elections of 1895 and 1900, the Liberals were very aware that the LRC could split the working-class vote in many constituencies. Soon after its inauguration, in 1902 and 1903 the LRC won two by-elections. In neither of these elections were the successful LRC candidates opposed by Liberals, and this emphasised the advantages that might accrue to Labour from an electoral agreement between the two parties not to contest particular seats. In 1903 an LRC candidate, Arthur Henderson of the Ironworkers, who had once worked as a Liberal election agent, beat both Conservatives and Liberals to win a by-election at Barnard Castle. This clearly made the point that the Liberals might also stand to gain from an electoral arrangement with the LRC in those areas where the LRC could be a real competitor. In Parliament the five LRC members already acted closely with the Lib-Labs, and a working agreement between the parties to defeat the Conservatives seemed a logical extension of this, even if it was not popular with the socialist 'rank and file' of the ILP.

In 1903 Ramsay MacDonald negotiated an electoral agreement with the Liberal Chief Whip, Herbert Gladstone (the youngest son of W.E. Gladstone). By this, the Liberals agreed not to contest a number of seats at the next general election. In return, it was agreed that the successful LRC Members of Parliament would support a Liberal government. The issue of an alliance with the Liberals was sufficiently sensitive for Hardie and MacDonald to keep the arrangement a secret from the rest of the LRC, even to the extent of denying its existence. This was to be only the first of a number of instances in the Labour Party's history when pragmatism and principle parted company. In the event, the LRC gained greatly from the pact, and 29 of its candidates including Hardie, Phillip Snowden, and Ramsay MacDonald, were successful in the general election of 1906. This group in Parliament now adopted the name, Labour Party, and elected Hardie its Chairman.

The election was a landslide victory for the Liberals, who secured 400 seats. This was largely the result of Conservative disarray over the issue of tariff reform. Their plan for abandoning free trade and intro- ducing protective tariffs would have, by their own admission, put a farthing on the cost of a loaf of bread. It proved relatively easy for the Liberals to campaign against the Conservatives' commitment to dearer food. In Parliament, under the Liberal Prime Minister, Campbell-Bannerman (and after 1908, Asquith), the Labour and Liberal parties worked together. The first fruit of this relationship was the Trades Disputes Act of 1906, which restored the unions' immunity to civil action and the right to peaceful picketing, which Taff Vale had thrown into doubt. A Workmen's Compensation Act in the same year established the right to compensation for accidents at work.

Although traditionally the advocates of the free market and *laissez-faire,* the Liberals now accepted that they needed to introduce social reform in order to deal with some of the most pressing problems of the day. Under the influence of Joseph Chamberlain, the Liberal Party had begun to re-think its position on social reform in the 1870s. The 'New Liberalism' attempted to create an interventionist role for the state whilst still retaining a primary commitment to private enter- prise. By the end of the nineteenth century it was clear that for the Liberals to thrive they had to develop this aspect of their policies. Social problems were obviously growing. A large proportion of the men who had volunteered to fight in the Boer War had been found to be unfit for service as a result of poor physical health. This raised questions about the ability of Britain to compete militarily with nations such as Germany, where welfare provision was undertaken by the state. At home, the Labour Party looked set to emerge as the party of social reform, and, given the Liberals' reliance on the working-class vote, this constituted a major threat.

In response, the Liberal government introduced a series of welfare reforms between 1906 and 1914. The Education (Provision of Meals) Act of 1906 enabled local authorities to provide school meals from the rates. Old Age Pensions were introduced in 1908, and in 1909 a system of voluntary labour exchanges was established to assist the unemployed. A National Insurance Act in 1911 made it compulsory for both employers and employees to contribute to a government fund from which benefit could be paid in the event of sickness or unemployment.

The 'new Liberalism' of the period after 1906 carried with it many of the social attitudes of the 'old Liberalism'. There was, for example, the same insistence that the working class consisted of two distinct groups – the respectable working class and the rest (the undeserving and deserving poor). The reforms were really aimed at the 'respectable' working class. The Old Age Pensions, for example, were not payable to anybody who, it was adjudged, had 'habitually' failed to work for their own maintenance. Also excluded were those who had been imprisoned for any offence in the ten years prior to their claim. This included anyone imprisoned as a result of involvement in strikes and political activity, and was designed as a control on working-class behaviour. Similarly, the introduction of national insurance was directed exclusively at those in work and did nothing for the unemployed. It also contained a contributory element, rather than providing benefit by right. The overall aim of the reform was to save the 'respectable' worker from sinking into the 'residuum', and to detach him from the appeal of the Labour Party. For example, in 1909 Winston Churchill, President of the Board of Trade in the Liberal Government, explained the thinking behind workmen's insurance:

> The idea is to increase the stability of our institutions by giving the mass of industrial workers a direct interest in maintaining them. With a 'stake in the country' in the form of insurance against evil days these workers will pay no attention to the vague promises of revolutionary socialism.

But, whatever Churchill imagined, the industrial workers were hardly being offered 'revolutionary socialism' at this time. With only 30 MPs, and the Liberals in reforming mood, the new Labour Party found it very difficult to make a distinctive mark on the House of Commons after the initial successes of 1906. Labour distinguished itself from the Liberals, not so much by its policies, but rather by its ability to see things from a distinctly working-class perspective. Despite their Lib-Lab MPs the Liberals remained a predominantly middle-class party with values and attitudes to match. This difference of perspective between the parties was demonstrated rather well in the response from Will Crooks, a cooper by trade and the Labour member for Woolwich, during the debate on Old Age Pensions in 1908. Conjuring up the orthodox belief that poverty was often self-inflicted, the Liberals proposed to exclude the 'drunken' from benefit. Crooks asked sarcastically: 'What particular degree of drunkenness was to disqualify for a pension? – half stewed, half drunk, steadily drunk, talkatively drunk, quarrelsome drunk, maudlin drunk, dead drunk?'. As he pointed out, drunkenness was not unknown at Westminster.

The real problem for the Labour Party, between 1906 and the outbreak of the war in 1914, lay in translating this distinctive working-class viewpoint into a clear political programme. In fact, up to 1914 there was little to distinguish the policy of the Labour Party from that of the Liberals. This was hardly surprising since many of the Labour members had supported the Liberal Party until fairly recently. This, and the importance to the young party of retaining the support of moderate trade unionists, militated against the adoption of overtly socialist policies. But the issue became a source of intense debate within the Labour Party. In 1908 Ben Tillett, hero of the dock strike and a member of the ILP, published a pamphlet entitled *Is the Parliamentary Labour Party a Failure?*, and it was widely read. Most of the pressure on the party to move to the left and to adopt a socialist programme came from the ILP, which continued to exist as a distinct organisation within the Labour Party. In 1910, frustrated by four years of living in the parliamentary shadow of the Liberals, a group in the ILP produced the so called 'green manifesto' *Let us Reform the Labour Party*. This called for more overtly socialist policies and a shared platform with the SDF.

But the Labour Party resisted the calls to adopt a more clearly socialist stance. If anything, with the affiliation in 1909 of the Miners' Federation with its Lib-Lab traditions, the party moved further away from socialism. For one thing, the alliance with the Liberals still paid concrete dividends. In the general election of January 1910 the Labour Party fielded 70 candidates, of whom 40 were successful. None of these had been opposed by a Liberal, and the secret electoral arrangement was clearly still in place. In the event, a second election was necessary later in 1910. The House of Lords refused to pass the 'people's budget', which the Chancellor of the Exchequer, Lloyd George, had designed to pay for the Liberal welfare reforms. Pushed by Labour, the Liberals decided on a constitutional reform to limit the veto of the Upper House, and dissolved Parliament in December 1910 to seek a mandate from the country for this reform. In this second election, 42 Labour members were returned.

Labour was still growing as a parliamentary force but the growth was painfully slow, and its record in by-elections was poor. There was no sign, before 1914, that Labour was destined to replace the Liberals as the second major party by 1924. At no election before 1918 did Labour secure more than 7.6 per cent of the vote nationally. Of course, not all working men were entitled to vote: some 40 per cent were still disenfranchised by the registration clauses attached to the Reform Act of 1884. But the harsh reality for Labour in this period was that most working people who possessed the franchise still voted for the other two parties, and mostly for the Liberals. Labour's weakness in Westminster derived from this fact.

The difficulties facing the new party in establishing a basis of mass support were demonstrated by its unsuccessful attempts to establish a distinctly Labour press. The *Daily Citizen*, launched in 1912 with the financial backing of the Labour Party and the TUC, failed by 1915. Its mistake lay in attempting to compete with the well-established popular papers such as the *Daily Mail*. With a readership of nearly a million, and funds to match, the *Mail* was more than equal to the challenge of the under-funded *Citizen*. Those on the left of the party argued that the paper suffered from the same problem as the Labour Party generally: it was too much like the existing products to establish itself fully with the customers. The *Daily Herald*, also launched in 1912, saw its role rather differently. Its target audience was the left of the party, seeing itself as a socialist news-sheet for the committed reader, and for this reason it survived while the more ambitious *Daily Citizen*, aiming at a far wider readership, went under. The *Herald* was edited by George Lansbury, who was assisted by Ben Tillett. Like so many of Labour's leading lights, Lansbury had once been a working-class member of the Liberal Party. He left in 1892 to join the SDF and in 1910 was elected Labour MP for Poplar, Bow and Bromley in the East End of London. Discouraged by the party's lukewarm support for female suffrage, he dramatically resigned his seat in 1912 and forced a by-election on the issue. Although he lost to a Conservative, his stand made him a hero of the Labour left. Under his editorship the *Daily Herald* constantly criticised Labour in parliament for compromising with the Liberals. The paper also supported the growth of militant trade unionism.

Although more enduring than the *Citizen*, the *Herald* suffered severe financial difficulties. Tillett revealed that at one point the editorial board arranged to have the office furniture bolted to the floor to prevent its sequestration by debt collectors. The Labour press remained as financially fragile as the Labour Party itself.

The vulnerability of the new party, with little funding outside that provided by the unions, was ably demonstrated by the Osborne Judgement of 1909. A member of the Amalgamated Society of Railway Servants objected to paying the political levy, that part of a member's subscription by which affiliated unions supported the Labour Party. The courts, backed again by the House of Lords, ruled that it was illegal for unions to compel members to pay a political levy. This hit the funds of the Labour Party badly, whilst leaving the other parties virtually unscathed. Labour now found itself relying on the Liberals to legislate against the ruling. In 1911 the Liberals introduced an Act to provide salaries for MPs for the first time. This went part way towards rectifying the problem, but Labour had to wait until the Trade Union Act of 1913 before the Osborne Judgement was reversed. All of this reinforced Labour's parliamentary dependence on the Liberals. In 1913 Phillip Snowden lamented that:

> The present labour representation in Parliament is there mainly by the goodwill of the Liberals, and it will disappear when that goodwill is turned into active resentment.

Historians tend to take one of two views of Labour's performance in Parliament before the First World War. Those on the left invariably indict the party for turning its back on a socialist programme. The same point was made repeatedly at the time by Lansbury's *Daily Herald,* as is shown in the cartoon reproduced on page 131. Ralph Miliband, in his book *Parliamentary Socialism* relates this firmly to the origins of the party. The socialism of the ILP lacked the cutting edge of continental socialism, partly because many of its supporters were

'A Fantasy', *Daily Herald*, 3 December 1913. The *Herald*'s cartoonist presents
Labour MPs bowing down to the interests of Capital, as depicted by the top
hat. It clearly demonstrates for us the difficulty the Labour Party had, of
maintaining a moderate and 'socialistic' stance, whilst being criticised by its
own left wing for not being socialist enough.

ex-Liberals. Yet even the mild socialism of the ILP was diluted by the
formation of the LRC and the need to placate the trade unions.
Labour's parliamentary impotence, he argues, was a logical out-
growth of its failure to develop its distinctiveness through a socialist
programme. Ramsay MacDonald seems to epitomise this failure,
moving from the Liberals to the ILP in 1894, and on to become
Secretary of the LRC in 1900 and leader of the Parliamentary party in
1911. MacDonald's view was that: 'Socialism is to come through a
socialistic political party and not a socialist one.' Other historians
have been less convinced of the potential appeal of an explicitly
socialist platform to the working-class voter. In his biography of
MacDonald, for example, David Marquand depicts a man, somewhere
between an idealist and a political realist, attempting to nurture support for a new and growing party by demonstrating its fitness to
govern. Since the mass appeal of socialism was at best unproven, the
Labour Party's only realistic strategy initially was to attach itself to the
Liberals, and to push for gradual reform.
  The interpretations of historians to some extent reflect the stra-
tegic options open to Labour in Parliament at the time: to back the
Liberals or to plough their own socialist furrow. After 1910 another

strategic option appeared. The failure of the Liberals to deal with contemporary social problems was reflected in another 'explosion' of trade union activity. This, and the growth of a militant women's movement claiming the right to vote, represented the re-birth of direct action. Its appearance, as an expression of discontent, was an indictment of Labour's parliamentary ineffectiveness and, inevitably, it challenged the parliamentary initiative as the way forward. But if the Labour Party felt threatened by the growth of militant extra-parliamentary protest, it was the 'new Liberalism' that was the main casualty. By 1914 it had been shown to be inadequate to meet the problems of British society and the post-war Labour Party was to be the main beneficiary of the Liberals' difficulties.

2 Labour Unrest 1910–14

> **KEY ISSUES** Why did trade union militancy increase so dramatically in 1910–14? How did this impact on the position of Liberals and Labour in parliament?

The table below, based on statistics kept by the Board of Trade, gives some idea of the growth of both the unions and industrial militancy in the period leading up to the First World War.

From this it can be seen that membership of trade unions fell slightly between the Taff Vale judgement of 1901 and the Trades Disputes Act of 1906. This decline led more unions to back the moves towards parliamentary representation for Labour. After 1906 the

	Trade union membership	Number of strikes	Number of strikers
1900	2,022,000	648	135,145
1901	2,025,000	642	111,437
1902	2,013,000	442	116,824
1903	1,994,000	387	93,515
1904	1,967,000	354	56,060
1905	1,997,000	358	57,653
1906	2,210,000	486	157,872
1907	2,513,000	601	100,728
1908	2,485,000	399	223,969
1909	2,477,000	436	170,258
1910	2,565,000	531	385,085
1911	3,134,000	903	831,104
1912	3,416,000	857	1,233,016
1913	4,135,000	1497	515,037
1914	4,145,000	972	326,000

unions grew, with a great increase in membership between 1910 and 1914. The columns showing the numbers of strikes and strikers respectively, make the same point, and suggest that 1912 was a crisis year with well over a million workers on strike at one time or another. The immediate cause of this period of unrest was the fall in real wages after 1900. This, in turn, was the result of declining productivity and comparatively low industrial investment as Britain's difficulties in the international market became increasingly apparent. In Britain's leading heavy industries prices increased and profits fell. The first sign of the malaise occurred in the cotton textile industry, the scene of relative industrial harmony since 1893 when the Brooklands collective bargaining machinery had been established. In 1908 the industry suffered a seven-week strike when the employers lowered wages. This was an indication of things to come, and in 1910 a strike wave broke on British industry. It focused initially on the coal mines of South Wales, particularly the Rhondda Valley, where a dispute grew up over payment for miners working difficult, or abnormal, seams.

The miners were angry, not only at the owners' attempts to reduce their wages, but also at the failure of their union leaders to protect them from such moves. The temperature of industrial conflict was clearly rising, with extensive clashes between the police and strikers, which left one striker dead and many injured at Tonypandy in 1911. In June 1911 the seamen went on strike and dock workers and railwaymen came out in sympathy. In August two strikers were shot dead by troops in Liverpool as general rioting broke out. In the same week troops shot dead two men, part of a crowd attacking a train at Llanelli. In 1912 the first ever national pit strike broke out, running from February to April. There were strikes in the London docks and among transport workers. 1913 brought strikes in the Midlands metal-working industries and a major strike of transport workers in Dublin.

It is the sheer scale of the numbers involved in the industrial disputes of these years that is remarkable. This was really the culmination of the movement towards larger, confederated organisations that had been taking place on both sides of industry for nearly 30 years. It also indicated a growth of trade unionism among the unskilled. As we have seen, moves had been made in this direction during the last great 'explosion' of industrial conflict between 1889 and 1893. Yet, by 1910 still only 17 per cent of workers were members of unions. The years from 1910 to 1914 saw a drawing in of many previously unorganised groups, so that by 1914 25 per cent of the workforce were members of unions. Women were prominent among the new recruits. In 1904 there had been 126,000 women in trade unions but by 1913 this had increased to 431,000. At this point women made up 10 per cent of all trade unionists.

This explosion of trade unionism was essentially a movement of the rank and file, with strikes growing directly from the shop floor. Even where the established unions were involved many of the strikes consisted of 'unofficial' action by rank and file trade unionists, acting without the consent of their central union leadership. Union officials often complained that they were the last to know that a strike was taking place. Many observers noted that these strikes seemed qualitatively different from earlier disputes, in that grievances were often imprecisely spelled out; strikers frequently took action and decided afterwards what the dispute was actually about.

In this way the period represented a crisis for the unions, confronting them with the problem of how to control the actions of their members. It also created difficulties for the Labour Party since the focus of action now shifted from Westminster to the workplace, away from reformism and towards direct action. Above all, the strike wave was an expression of discontent with the existing strategies for advancing Labour's case, collective bargaining in the industrial sphere and parliamentary support for moderate social reform in the political sphere. The promised benefits of these two strategies had not materialised. Neither had been able to prevent the fall in real wages and the deterioration of working conditions. In the main, working people were unimpressed by the Liberal reforms. Declining wages and increasing job insecurity seemed to outweigh the benefits of any welfare legislation.

Troops and the police were used to combat strikes in this period to a far greater extent than ever before. The confrontations on the streets made it easy to see the strike movement in revolutionary terms. The threat to the overall stability of society was emphasised by the role played by the ideas of Syndicalism. These were most popularly associated with the French left-wing political thinker Georges Sorel, whose book *Reflections on Violence* was published in 1905, following the author's observation of French trade unions *(syndicats)* in action. The Syndicalists turned their backs on political action and argued that the trade union could be the basis of a society run by the workers. Instead of sectional unions concerned with this or that detail of a particular trade, unions should amalgamate and act together. The ultimate aim was to stop society dead by a general strike that would paralyse the nation and precipitate a transfer of power to the unions. The Syndicalists advocated class warfare and direct action, believing that every strike acted to increase the class awareness of the participants.

In Britain this approach was advocated by a journal called *The Syndicalist*, edited by Tom Mann, rekindling the direct action of 'new unionism'. Mann was imprisoned in 1912 for inciting the troops, who confronted the strikers, to mutiny. From his cell he explained the aims and antecedents of syndicalism:

1 Syndicalism means the control of industry by 'Syndicates' or Unions of Workers, in the interests of the entire community. ... Robert Owen, over eighty years ago, advocated the necessity for such a method of organization, ... Since Owen's time, several other methods have been
5 resorted to by the workers to escape from their industrial bondage, but none of them have proved really effective, parliamentary action least of all.

Another familiar figure, Ben Tillett, fostered syndicalism among the dock workers. In South Wales the miners were led by men such as A.J. Cook, who had previously been active in the local branches of the ILP but was frustrated by its commitment to parliamentary reformism. In 1912 Cook and others published an influential pamphlet called *The Miners' Next Step*. In this they criticised the mining unions for their reliance on collective bargaining and advocated a fully integrated union of all coal miners that would take over and run the mines. The impact of this approach, and the challenge it constituted to the Labour Party's reformist strategy, may be seen in the comments of a rank and file South Wales miner, the Baptist lay preacher Arthur Horner, on reading this pamphlet:

1 This programme and the movement it created throughout the coalfield gave me the inspiration I had been looking for ... The conception of working-class power was to me far more realistic than the idea of fighting for seats in Parliament merely for supporters of the Liberal-Labour
5 alliance.

Certainly, Labour in Parliament saw the re-birth of industrial militancy as weakening its position. Ramsay MacDonald called syndicalism 'the impatient frenzied, thoughtless child of poverty, disappointment [and] irresponsibility'. Similarly, George Barnes, a former general secretary of the ASE, and now a Labour member for Glasgow, poured scorn on the new approach:

1 There are, however, some Labour leaders of anarchical proclivities who are leading newly organised labour into the ditch by strikes. They have become obsessed in favour of the strike policy, and in order to make it more attractive they present it in a fancy name imported from France.
5 ... That I say is fool's talk. I for one will be no party to a policy of that kind, because I know that nothing but disaster can come of it. ... To talk of a general strike as a policy for organised Labour is sheer madness.

In fact, it is easy to exaggerate the importance of the Syndicalists. Their direct influence was less than they would have wished. The labour unrest of these years grew from the grass roots rather than being imported in the form of new ideas from the Continent. The Syndicalists simply tried to harness this movement. One of the government's arbitrators, George Askwith, appointed under the 1896 Conciliation Act, concluded that 'it looks as if we are in the presence of one of those periodic upheavals in the labour world such as occurred in 1833–4, and from time to time since that date'. Askwith was right, there was much in this outburst of trade unionism that recalled the 'Plug disturbances' of 1842, or the advent of general unionism in 1889. Yet this particular 'periodic upheaval' was to have a lasting impact on trade unionism, both by extending union organisation among the unskilled and by the development of the 'sympathy' strike on behalf of other trades. Many of the disputes had taken this form, and this was reflected in the establishment of the Triple Alliance between the Miners, the Railway-men and the Transport Workers in 1914. By this pact (celebrated by the *Daily Herald*'s cartoonist), the unions in three major industries agreed to take sympathetic action if any one of them was in dispute. Through this agreement the legacy of the pre-war period of unrest would be felt in the General Strike of 1926.

For the moment it was clear that, in the light of Labour's disappointing showing at Westminster, a large section of the working community had put its faith in extra-parliamentary action. The Liberal government, under Asquith, now sought to underpin the Labour Party as an alternative (and more acceptable) medium for working-class aspirations. Thus in 1911 it brought in its measure, introducing wages for MPs and, by the Trade Union Act of 1913, reversing the Osborne judgement. This made it legal for unions to levy their members to support the Labour Party. Nevertheless, the growth of extra-

'Union of Trade Unions is Strength', *Daily Herald*, 23 April 1914. The miners, railway and transport workers signalled in 1911 that they would be willing to work together to create a general strike under certain circumstances. This was later embodied in the Triple Alliance of 1914. Here the pact is celebrated by the *Herald*'s cartoonist as a combined force that could not be broken by Capital (note the top hat again). The events of the General Strike of 1926 were to prove this assumption deeply mistaken.

parliamentary action was a forcible reminder that, under the registration clauses of the last Reform Act, about 40 per cent of men were still unenfranchised. The Liberals also found themselves under pressure to extend the electorate to include women.

In 1903 Emmeline Pankhurst, the widow of a prominent Liberal barrister, left the ILP to form the Women's Social and Political Union. This became the focus of the Suffragette movement calling for 'votes for women'. Pankhurst had despaired of persuading the Labour Party to adopt female suffrage in its policies. She now turned to direct action as a way of putting pressure on the Liberal government. The WSPU grew as a movement of mainly middle-class women. Within the Labour Party the call for female suffrage was led by the women textile trade unionists from Lancashire, who were supported by the ILP, but with little initial success. Between 1900 and 1912 annual female suffrage resolutions to both the TUC and the Labour Party Conference were voted out by the, predominantly male, representatives. The TUC saw women as unskilled labour threatening the jobs of skilled men. The Labour Party argued that any campaign to extend the vote should address the registration anomalies that still excluded 40 per cent of working men. But behind these highly pragmatic arguments lay an acceptance by the working man of the mid-Victorian dictum that a woman should be the 'angel in the house'. Perhaps more than any other single issue this demonstrates how close Labourism was to Liberalism at this time. Hannah Mitchell, a working woman active with the ILP in Lancashire, found men in the labour movement very unsympathetic,

> Even as Socialists they seldom translate their faith into works, being still conservatives at heart, especially where women are concerned. Most of us who were married found that 'Votes for Women' were of less interest to our husbands than their own dinners.

It was not until 1912 that the Labour Party Conference, under pressure from the growing number of female trade unionists, accepted a female suffrage resolution, as did the TUC the following year. However, at this point world events overtook the Labour movement.

3 The Advent of War

KEY ISSUE How did the war change the relationship between Liberals and Labour in parliament?

In his book, *The Strange Death of Liberal England*, published in 1935, George Dangerfield argued that the outbreak of war in August 1914 saved Britain from a revolution. His case was that the labour unrest, combined with the Suffragette militancy and a revolt over Home Rule in Ulster, threatened the very stability of the state and left the Liberal Party in tatters. But this compellingly readable account of these years rather exaggerated the situation. In fact, the strikes were on the wane by the summer of 1914 and suffragette militancy seems to have 'peaked' even earlier. Nevertheless, the turmoil of the years from 1910 to 1914 seemed to carry two implications. First, that the Liberal Party had clearly been unable to deal with the problems which society faced in the early twentieth century. Liberal welfare reforms, constructed on the huge parliamentary majority of 1906, had not offset the growing alienation between the classes that seemed an increasingly evident feature of British life. Second, the re-birth of extra-parliamentary direct action seemed to be, at least partly, a result of the exclusion of a large segment of the population from participation in parliamentary politics. The social conflict of 1910–14 pressed the case eloquently for a radical extension of the franchise. In 1917 the Russian Revolution would provide a chilling model of what happened when direct action was taken to its logical conclusion.

These factors, and the participation of men and women in the war effort, ensured the future success of the young Labour Party. The Representation of the People Act of 1918 introduced full male suffrage for the first time. The registration clauses and mixed franchises of earlier Reform Acts were replaced by an altogether more accessible system that was no longer weighted against the interests of the working-class voter. Also, a first, if rather cautious, element of female suffrage was introduced. Women over 30 who were (or whose husbands were) ratepayers were now allowed to vote. This may have been 'votes for ladies' rather than 'votes for women', but the principle of a female parliamentary franchise had been conceded.

By 1922 the Labour Party had overtaken the Liberals as the nation's second major political party next to the Conservatives. The Liberals, divided amongst themselves, carried the stigma of their pre-war failure. On the other hand, the Labour Party emerged from the war with a fresh constitution and with experience of administration in the wartime coalition government. Offering itself as a party of government commanding a special relationship with the trade unions, it was well placed to pick up the new voters of a wider franchise, most of whom were working class. Its own origins in liberalism would continue to hamper its actions, and make the new constitution's commitment to the common ownership of the means of production a source of embarrassment to many of the party's leading figures. But the passing of the Liberal Party into irrevocable decline left the Labour Party as the party of the working class in Parliament.

Summary Diagram
Labour in Parliament 1902–14

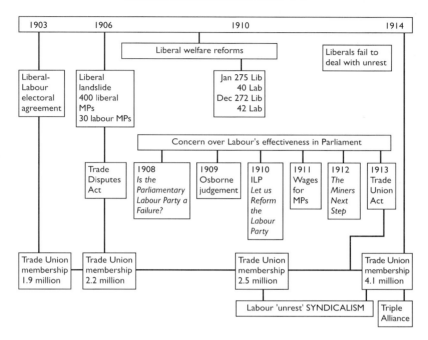

1903	1906	1910	1914

Liberal welfare reforms

Liberals fail to deal with unrest

Liberal-Labour electoral agreement

Liberal landslide 400 liberal MPs 30 labour MPs

Jan 275 Lib 40 Lab Dec 272 Lib 42 Lab

Concern over Labour's effectiveness in Parliament

Trade Disputes Act

1908 *Is the Parliamentary Labour Party a Failure?*

1909 Osborne judgement

1910 ILP *Let us Reform the Labour Party*

1911 Wages for MPs

1912 *The Miners Next Step*

1913 Trade Union Act

Trade Union membership 1.9 million

Trade Union membership 2.2 million

Trade Union membership 2.5 million

Trade Union membership 4.1 million

Labour 'unrest' SYNDICALISM

Triple Alliance

Working on Chapter 6

This chapter has shown how Labour's performance as a parliamentary party was always restricted by its origins in liberalism and trade unionism. The party's difficulties were compounded by a reforming Liberal Party and the rise of militant trade unionism. At this stage there was little to suggest that Labour would take over from the Liberals as the second party. The following headings may help you to capture these points in your notes:

1. Labour and the Liberals. How well did Labour establish itself in this period in relation to the Liberals?
2. The growth of extra-parliamentary challenge. To what extent was this a consequence of Labour's performance to date, a) on labour unrest 1910–1914 b)on its policy towards female suffrage?
3. Labour in 1914: a party for the future? How well placed to supersede the Liberal Party did Labour appear to be in 1914?

The key to understanding the difficulties of the Labour Party in these years lies in appreciating the wide range of organisations and people who supported it. This included those from skilled trade unions, like the engineering workers, who had only recently left the Liberal Party, through to the ILP with its demand for a more overtly socialist programme. Labour had to steer its path between these two centrifugal forces.

Answering structured and essay questions on Chapter 6

Most essay questions on the Labour Party in this period concentrate on the mixed origins of the party and its relative weakness in these early years. They invariably involve examining the pressures towards disunity that were consequent upon drawing support from a range of organisations, as well as Labour's continuing reliance on the Liberals in Parliament before 1914.

Here is an example of a structured question on the rise of the Labour Party:

a) What were the factors leading to the establishment by Keir Hardie of the Independent Labour Party (ILP) in 1893? (*5 marks*)
b) Why did trade unions' support for a separate working-class party increase from 1900 to 1914? (*5 marks*)
c) How successful was the Labour Party in achieving its aims before 1914? (*10 marks*)

Part a) asks you to collect together the various elements that were particularly dissatisfied with the representation offered by the Liberal Party, and you have the opportunity to refer to the Socialist Clubs, the Nonconformist element, the leadership of men like Hardie and Snowden, and the involvement of some trade unions (notably the Textile Workers). Part b) gives the opportunity to chart the growth of trade union support before and after Taff Vale and into the syndicalist period. Part c) asks you to make a judgement on how far Labour achieved its aim of providing a distinctive 'socialistic' voice for the working-class voter (here you should bear in mind the tensions between the 'reformist' and the socialist elements of the party).

Here are some examples of the way essay questions may be framed:

1. Explain why a distinct Labour Party was formed by 1906.
2. How important a force was the Labour Party in British Politics before 1914?
3. To what extent was the emergence of the Labour Party a result of the growing strength of the trade unions in the second half of the nineteenth century?
4. 'Trade unionist rather than socialist'. Discuss this view of the Labour Party before 1914.
5. What movements combined to form the Labour Party, and how united and effective was that party in the period up to 1914?

6. 'Socialist neither in its origins nor its policies.' Do you agree with this comment on the Labour Party before 1914?

7. 'Keir Hardie, rather than the trade unions, deserves the credit for the emergence of the Labour Party.' How far do you agree with this view?

There are three focal points in these questions: i) the relative import-ance of trade unionism in the emergence of Labour; ii) the parlia-mentary impact of Labour before the war; and iii) the extent to which Labour should be seen as a socialist party in this period. The empha-sis on each of these issues varies from question to question and you will need to decide which should have priority. Yet all involve an appreciation of the support that Labour relied upon.

Question 7 provides a useful reminder that in looking at the emergence of the Party long- and short-term causes should be ident-ified (in this case did Hardie create his own context for action or did he respond to a context created by broader social and economic fac-tors?). Remember that questions on Labour's parliamentary per-formance invariably involve some consideration of the position of the other parties (strengths and weaknesses), particularly the Liberals in their role as Labour's major competitor for working-class votes. Here your judgements on what the Labour Party achieved must be bal-anced by an understanding of what could reasonably have been expected of it given the nature of its support.

You will also need to explore the issue of the support the party drew upon in answering questions on the extent to which Labour was 'socialist' in its approach. Questions on Labour's ideological prove-nance tend to be posed in a polemical form as questions 4 and 6 above demonstrate. The *polemical question* (a question to which there appears to be only one answer, and that contained within the ques-tion itself) is much beloved by examiners and it is a style that can be confusing. The quotations used always seem to come from a world of cast iron certainties, whereas the historical circumstances you find yourself addressing rarely seem to lend themselves to such definite statements. However, you should try not to allow a dogmatic state-ment in the question to lead you to an answer that considers only one perspective. Given the broad range of ideas and institutions involved in the early Labour Party it seems likely that a question such as number 6 will be best answered with an essay arguing that 'in these ways and to this extent it was/but in these ways and to this extent it was not'.

Source-based questions on Chapter 6

1 Tom Mann in *The Syndicalist* and George Barnes on Syndicalism.

Read these very different accounts of syndicalism on pages 134 and 135 carefully. Answer the following questions:

a) Why does Mann quote Robert Owen in his explanation of syndicalism? (*2 marks*)

b) What were the seeming advantages of syndicalism over other methods that could have been adopted by working people to improve their condition? (*5 marks*)

c) In what ways was Barnes scornful of syndicalism? (4 marks)

d) Why was Barnes, a trade unionist himself, so set against a general strike? (*3 marks*)

e) How far do these extracts illustrate the weaknesses of the Labour movement in the early twentieth century? (*10 marks*)

2 Cartoons from the *Daily Herald*.

Carefully examine these cartoons on pages 131 and 136 and describe what is happening in each of them so as to make clear their meaning. (*7 marks*)

Answer the following questions:

a) With what justification did the cartoonist caricature Labour in Parliament in the cartoon entitled 'A Fantasy'? (*4 marks*)

b) Compare these cartoons with the documentary extracts that you examined in question 1 on the previous page, and consider what position Mann and Barnes might have taken on the issues depicted in the cartoons. (*4 marks*)

7 Conclusion. Labour and Reform 1815–1914: Achievements and Failures

POINTS TO CONSIDER

Should the working-class movements that emerged in the century after 1815 be judged to have succeeded or to have failed? Above all, have historians succeeded in writing the history of these movements in a way that recognises and respects the working-class voice?

KEY DATES

1819	Peterloo Massacre.
1832	First Reform Act.
1839/42/48	Rejection of first, second and third Chartist petitions.
1867	Second Reform Act; establishment of the Trade Union Congress.
1884	Third Reform Act.
1906	Formation of the Labour Party.
1918	Representation of the People Act.
1918	General Election – Labour take 22% of the total vote.

The Representation of the People Act of 1918 extended the electorate from its pre-war figure of around eight million to a massive 21 million voters. For the first time the electoral system gave the effective right to vote to all men over the age of 21. Plural voting, which distorted the electoral system in favour of the middle class, was greatly reduced. The 1918 Act also introduced a limited female suffrage, and this would be extended in 1928 to give women the vote on the basis of equality with men. Moves were also made in the 1918 legislation to equalise the numbers of voters in constituencies. The single member constituency with a population of around 70,000 was seen to be the norm. Although there continued to be some variation throughout the country, the massive inequalities in distribution that had previously marked the constituency system were ironed out. In addition, voters in receipt of poor relief were no longer disenfranchised.

It had taken over a century of pressure and protest to convert a parliamentary system based on property and influence into a mass democracy. Along the way the nature of politics had changed markedly. Members of Parliament were now seen as the representatives of people rather than of 'interests', as had been the case in 1832. Party organisation was now more significant than at any time before; since politics was geared to the demands of a mass electorate, support had to be maintained so that it could be effectively mobilised at election time. Politics had also become more adversarial in a number of ways. The maximum period between general elections was reduced from seven years to five in 1911, so elections occurred more frequently. The number of uncontested seats dropped dramatically, from 163 in the election of December 1910, to a mere seven in 1929 and three in 1945. Also, this was an electorate that was active in the use of its vote. The turnout in the general election of 1918 stood at 57.2 per cent of electors and rose to 73 per cent in the general election of 1922. It has never fallen below 70 per cent since then.

Undoubtedly, it was the working-class voter who benefited from these changes. The traditional fear of including the working man in the electoral system, which had accompanied the earlier Reform Acts, had been replaced during the labour unrest of 1910–14 by fear of the consequences of his continued exclusion. Yet how close was this mass democracy, in practice, to the vision of the Chartists in 1839? To put this another way, judged in terms of the aims of Chartism, how successful were working-class movements in the long run? By 1918, five of the Chartist's Six Points had been conceded. The one outstanding Chartist demand, for annual Parliaments, was never to be enacted and there is today no lobby for the achievement of this point. Yet for the Chartists, annual Parliaments would have been a central feature of a political system based on full participation and accountability. They envisaged that Parliament would reflect the 'will of the people' because the Members of Parliament would be constantly in touch with the people who elected them. In a system where elections take place every five years there can never be that same degree of contact, and the represented must, in consequence, give up some of their authority and control to their representative. Whilst voter turn-out at general elections remains high today, the citizens of a modern democracy are not actively involved in political decision-making as the Chartists argued that they should be in a healthy democracy.

It is also worth making the point that as far as radical movements are concerned the timing of concessions is always important. The Chartists wanted the Six Points in 1839, when an immature industrial system could be shaped, during its formation, to working-class needs. By 1918 the important features of an industrial society were in place and would never be altered. The Chartists, for example, saw labour as 'the source of all wealth' and felt that manual work should be seen to be as important as the work of the industrialist, the manager or the professional. By 1918 the distinction between 'blue collar' (or manual) labour and 'white collar' work was well established and continues to be reflected in the distribution of rewards in our society.

Perhaps the fact that we find annual Parliaments so difficult to contemplate provides a measure of the distance of our democratic system from that envisaged by the Chartists. They aspired to annual Parliaments because they felt that a longer period between elections would reduce the involvement of citizens in their own government. To some extent they have been proved correct. Today the 'average' voter is not a political activist. Yet for some historians the lack of a substantial involvement by most voters in modern-day politics has led them to doubt that Chartism ever attracted the massive support that other historians, such as Dorothy Thompson, claim for the movement in the 1830s and 1840s. For example Malcolm Thomis, in his book *The Town Labourer and the Industrial Revolution* (1974), makes assumptions about the Chartists based on the existence of, what he sees as, political apathy when he was writing, in the 1970s:

1   In spite of Aristotle, man continues to give ample evidence of his wish not to be a political animal, and experience of modern-day Labour politics at the ward level is a much more accurate guide to the nineteenth century than romantic dreams of frustrated revolution ... The failure of
5   Chartism exemplified all the weaknesses of the working class as a political force, a basic lack of interest in politics, fragmentation, and a preoccupation with sectional economic interests ...

Of course, this is one of our difficulties in trying to understand the Chartists and to write their history. How could so many working people have been energised, for so long and with such resilience, over political issues? But should historians judge the past in terms of the present in this rather mechanical way? Because politics occupies a particular place in our own society, does it necessarily follow that this is the place it has always occupied? One would not, for example, make assumptions about the importance of religion in the Middle Ages based on church attendance today. Chartism was able to engender huge support because it addressed an audience that thought and acted politically. Much of this changed with the defeat of Chartism, after which limited objectives, such as securing legal status for trade unions, seemed most likely to succeed. The Labour Party, in the early twentieth century, managed to make the idea of the parliamentary representation of working communities a reality. Yet measured against the Chartist vision of a country run largely by, and in the interests of, working people, the achievements of the Labour Party by 1914 inevitably look rather unimpressive.

However, it is perhaps unfair to indict the early Labour Party for not maintaining the idealistic goals of their predecessors, and for not achieving more than it did. As a result of the 'Labour alliance' strategy developed by Keir Hardie, working people were represented in Parliament by men of their own class who shared the same kinds of values and beliefs. Of course, the Labour Party would never be directly synonymous with the working class, since many working-class voters owed allegiance to the other parties. However, the vote com-

	Labour's % share of total vote in general elections
1900	1.8
1906	5.9
1910 (Jan)	7.6
1910 (Dec)	7.1
1918	22.2
1922	29.5
1923	30.5
1924	33.0
1929	37.1
1931	33.0
1935	37.9
1945	47.8

manded by Labour in the inter-war period, suggests a flourishing basis of support in working-class areas.

This increasing share of the electorate's support, and the fact that Labour governments were formed in 1924, 1929 and 1945, suggest that working-class political reform movements in the nineteenth and early twentieth century should be viewed as a huge success story. In 1924 Labour formed its first administration, a minority government that would last only a matter of months. Nevertheless, this was a significant moment in political history; with the Conservatives unable to form an administration despite gaining the most seats, Labour, rather than the Liberals, were the alternative party of government.

On 22 January 1924, Ramsay MacDonald met King George V and accepted his appointment as Prime Minister. Historian Ralph Miliband points out that the King entered this interview with some trepidation for he feared, wrongly, that MacDonald really was the extreme socialist that he was portrayed as being in the Conservative press. The king's thoughts turned to his grandmother, Queen Victoria, whose reign had spanned two Reform Acts and the Chartist movement. 'Today 23 years ago', he confided to his diary, 'dear Grandmamma died, I wonder what she would have thought of a Labour government'. His remarks pointed to the real achievement of the early Labour Party; it had made possible, what had been unthinkable throughout the nineteenth century, a government made up of men predominantly from the working class.

In the event, the King and Ramsay MacDonald got along splendidly, as one might expect of two moderates, both keen to maintain the peace of the realm and the stability of its institutions. When the king told MacDonald that he deplored the reported singing of the 'Red Flag' at a recent Labour Party meeting, the Labour leader sympathised. But he asked the king to appreciate 'the very difficult position he was in *vis-a-vis* to his own extremists'. The juggling act that MacDonald was clearly very conscious of performing at this point involved steering the party between its two classic strategies of reformism and direct action. There were those who welcomed the call for Labour to form a government as an opportunity to enact real socialist legislation, even at the expense of precipitating a further general election and Labour's fall from office. On the other hand there were those, and MacDonald was one, who saw this as the moment for Labour to act the statesman and to demonstrate the Party's capacity to rule. Rather than introducing radical change, a Labour government should show that it could hold the reins of power, at home and abroad, in a way that was credible.

This is the choice that has dogged the Labour Party since its earliest days, with the 'idealists' emphasising socialist principles and the 'realists' stressing that Party policy must be constrained by what is politically possible. All radical movements have to decide, at some point in their history, whether there is more to be gained by conciliation than by conflict. In this book we identified this choice in operation in the case of the Chartists (rejecting revolutionary solutions in the wake of Newport), the early trade unionists (opting to push for 'respectable' legal status after 1850) and the Labour Party (opposing the direct action of Syndicalism).

For the Labour Party the choice between directly confronting the capitalist system or alternatively working within it to bring about gradual change, has always been complicated by the relationship with the trade unions. As we have seen, the party grew as the political arm of the trade union movement. Yet when trade unions are militant it has always been hard for the Labour Party to project itself convincingly as a party of government. For this reason the parliamentary Labour Party was deeply embarrassed by the labour unrest before the First World War, and later by the General Strike of 1926. To put this another way, there was always a problem for Labour as a parliamentary party, in that it drew support and funding from organisations which periodically expressed themselves in extra-parliamentary ways. A reformist Labour Party is always likely, therefore, to encourage moderate trade unionism with an emphasis on collective bargaining. Significantly, Labour's return to power in the 1990s, after the Thatcher years, came at a time when trade unionism was not a very effective force.

1 History from Below

> **KEY ISSUES** How did the participants in the early Labour Party write the history of nineteenth century working-class movements, and how influential has that been to our own view of those movements?

It has always been important for radical movements to write their own history as part of the process of establishing their own identity. The Chartists constantly referred to historical precedent to justify their demands. In fact, their case for the inclusion of working men in the electorate was predominantly argued on historical grounds. Thomas Paine, as we saw in Chapter 2, hypothesised that at one time, the 'free born Englishman' had enjoyed all the freedom to which the Chartists would later aspire, but that these had been removed by William the Conqueror in 1066. Similarly, Major John Cartright, founder of the Hampden Clubs after 1812, claimed that these 'freedoms' had been verified by a written Saxon constitution. The Chartists always argued that working people wanted a *restoration* of their ancient rights, rather than the creation of new rights. In the last chapter we saw Tom Mann justifying Syndicalism by referring to Robert Owen. In the same way, when the civil rights movement grew in the United States in the 1960s and 1970s under the leadership of Martin Luther King and Black Power groups, one of their first demands was that black history be included in the nation's educational curriculum. A sense of the past has always been an essential requisite for any movement attempting to bring about change in the present.

Most of the early assessments of the history of the Labour Party were sympathetic. This is partly because most of the earliest historians of working-class movements were themselves active in the Labour Party. The first histories of Chartism, for example, were all written from within the reformist Labour tradition in the early twentieth century, and tended to stress the continuities between the early radical movements and the rise of the Labour Party. In this way the earlier movements became part of the pedigree of the new party and were presented as first faltering steps on the road to the Labour Party.

However, the need to use the past to justify actions in the present does not always produce good history. Most commonly it establishes false continuities between movements with few real links. Take, for example, Francis Williams' *Fifty Years March* (1949), a history of the Labour Party writtenby a leading member of the ILP. In this work the *whole* of British history was seen as a progress towards Clement Attlee's Labour government of 1945. As Williams put it:

1   The history of socialism in Britain goes back through the soil of the centuries to the early peasants' revolts against the enclosure of the common lands, to the Christian communism of John Wycliff, to John Ball ... The history moves to Jack Cade and the revolt of the Kentish
5   peasants ... It becomes vocal again in the voice of Milton's republicanism, in the demands of the Levellers in the war between Parliament and King ... – it is a thread that runs unbroken through British history.

Having established the antecedents of parliamentary socialism in the mediaeval and early modern periods the author then moves through the movements of the nineteenth century and on to the founding of the LRC in 1900, of which he comments, 'It is only rarely that history fully lives up to its spectacular possibilities'.

Not all of the work of the early labour historians was so mechanistic and excellent historical scholarship was often produced. Yet, even in the best of this work, the search for continuities between periods whose historical contexts were actually very different, was a common feature. This, of course, related to the fact that the historians were themselves part of the evolution of the Labour Party. Sidney and Beatrice Webb, whose *History of Trade Unionism* was published in 1894, were both members of the Fabian Society and founder members of the LRC. Sidney Webb was one of the authors of the Labour Party's new constitution, drawn up in 1918. G.D.H. Cole, who wrote a number of works examining the origins of working-class radicalism, was a member of the Labour Party and established the New Fabian Research Bureau in the 1930s to keep Labour MPs informed on the issues of the day. Among the best known of his books are *The Common People 1746–1946* (1938) and *Chartist Portraits* (1941). John and Barbara Hammond, also active members of the Fabians, concentrated their attention on the impact that early industrialisation had on particular groups of workers. Many of their books are still being reprinted today – among them, *The Town Labourer* (1925), *The Village Labourer* (1927) and *The Skilled Labourer* (1927). The work of the Webbs, Cole and the Hammonds established 'labour history' as a respectable area of study for historians. Previously, history had been almost exclusively concerned with the activities of statesmen, monarchs and the politically powerful. This was 'history from above'. In the early twentieth century it was argued that working people also had their history. The challenge of the new 'labour history' was to tell the story of the growth of an industrial society from the viewpoint of the working person. This was 'history from below'. The large amount of academic research which is now devoted to the history of working-class movements, and even the inclusion of such topics in modern-day examination syllabuses, is directly attributable to the work of these early pioneers.

Yet, it should always be remembered, that these formative influences on labour history derived from within the reformist tradition of the Labour Party in the early twentieth century. This determined the kind of interpretation that was offered. The heroes of the early labour histories tended to be those characters from the early movements who most seemed to be the forebears of the Labour Party with its commitment to gradualism. Characters, such as Feargus O'Connor, who did not fit easily into this mould, were drawn as the villains of labour history. O'Connor was soon written off as a 'hot-head', a mob orator who was unwilling to make the compromises necessary to achieve political success for the Chartist movement. G.D.H. Cole said of O'Connor that: 'He was, in truth, a disastrous leader', and this has become the orthodox judgement on him. Lovett, on the other hand, with his gradualist schemes of educating working people before giving them the vote, was regarded as a worthy forerunner of the twentieth-century Labour activists. In most of the early histories of Chartism, the movement's failure was attributed to its adhesion to the policies of O'Connor (considered a 'physical force' Chartist), and the movement's inability to identify the future possibilities that were present in the approach of Lovett (considered a 'moral force' Chartist). This is certainly the analysis adopted by Mark Hovell in his influential book, *The Chartist Movement,* published after his death in 1917. Hovell had been a lecturer in the Workers' Education Association, an organisation that grew from within the Labour Party and devoted itself to providing the education that working people still were not receiving from the state. Little wonder that Lovett, with his schemes for workers' education, was the hero of this account; one could easily imagine Lovett himself as a WEA lecturer. O'Connor, on the other hand, was seen to have frightened away any support that might have come from the middle class. 'O'Connor's speech', Hovell remarks on one occasion, 'was another example of indirect terrorism, intended to scare away the remaining moderates.

This division between 'moral force' and 'physical force', which the early labour historians claimed to have been so destructive to the fortunes of Chartism, was simply a projection back into history of the context within which the early Labour Party found itself in the first 30 years of this century. At this time labour movements were torn between reformism on the one hand, and the direct action of trade union militants on the other. In this context the history of Chartism was crafted by parliamentary socialists as a stern warning of what happens when radical movements want too much too soon and try to use force to get it. The message of most of these interpretations of the earlier working-class movements was that gradualism and the politics of conciliation are more productive in the long run than the strike, the public disturbance, or the revolutionary uprising. It is an interpretation that has proved to be very resilient.

Despite this, over the years there have been many on the left, writing 'history from below', who have argued the opposite case, that the commitment to parliamentary socialism closed down important options for the working community, and forced the labour movement to 'play the game' by the rules of a capitalist society. Historians taking this view feel that Labour lost as much as it gained in its movement into formal politics. The compromises with other parties, which the parliamentary system often involved, and the need to appeal to a predominantly moderate electorate, inevitably led to a heavily diluted form of socialism that perhaps was not socialism at all. From this point of view, the great failure of the labour movements after 1815 lies in the fact that the major institutions to which they gave rise, particularly the TUC and the Labour Party, acted to reinforce capitalism rather than bringing about its destruction.

It will always be impossible to reconcile the views of the 'idealists' and those of the 'political realists': those who argue that there should be no compromise with a corrupt system and those who believe that corrupt systems can be reformed gradually from within. This has always been a point of debate within radical movements and is also where labour historians reach their maximum point of disagreement. But whatever the differences of interpretation that are offered, there is a consensus among these historians on two points and it may be useful to close by stating them, since they form a large part of the approach taken in this book.

First, there is a general acceptance that a full appreciation of the growth of an industrial society *should* include an exploration of working-class movements for political and industrial reform. Without an account of the successes and failures of these movements the picture is incomplete in significant ways. Second, a feeling has grown up, since the first wave of labour histories written by active participants in the early Labour Party, that historians should aim to see working-class movements in their *own* terms, that is, through the eyes of the people who took part in them. This is perhaps best exemplified in the work of E.P. Thompson, particularly his *Making of the English Working Class* (1963). Both of these points have informed the writing of this book. It is hoped that the insights afforded into the experience of the participants have enabled us to put these movements into the context of their own time. The movements of protest that we have examined grew from the responses of ordinary people to the world around them and represent their attempts to influence the course of events. Their strategies and approaches differed from period to period and their achievements frequently did not match their aspirations. Thompson wrote in the 1960s, a time of great hope for the left in British and European politics. Much of the work of these years probably over-stresses class consciousness as a constant factor in British politics after 1832. As we have seen, some of the movements, like Chartism, did draw on class solidarities. Others, like the trade unions, tended to stress the diversity of the social groups that made up the working class. But it remains important to understand these movements in their own contexts because they consistently provided an alternative way of looking at the world to that which dominated their society. In this sense their failures may be as instructive to us as their successes.

Working on Chapter 7

Here you are concerned to arrive at a judgement on working-class movements in the period. You may find the following headings useful:

1. The situation in 1918.
2. The aims of Chartism and the achievements of the Labour Party.
3. History from below; the alternative interpretations.

Further Reading

Reference has been made at various points to **E.P. Thompson**, *The Making of the English Working Class* (Pelican, 1968 edn, first published 1963). This huge book has inspired controversy and a renewed interest in working-class movements among historians. A good flavour of its re-think of the impact of industrialisation on social relations can be derived from a reading of chapters 6–10. A useful alternative overview, from a liberal perspective, is **Harold Perkin**, *The Origins of Modern English Society 1780–1880* (Routledge and Kegan Paul, 1969). A good discussion of the issues raised by 'class' is available in **R.J. Morris**, *Class and Class Consciousness in the Industrial Revolution 1780–1850* (Methuen, 1979). The most recent interpretations of 'class' as an analytical tool for historians can be found in **Rohan McWilliam**, *Popular Politics in Nineteenth Century England* (Routledge, 1998).

The pre-Reform system has been reconsidered by **Frank O'Gorman**, *Voters, Patrons and Parties* (OUP, 1989) and he makes an important case for the representative nature of eighteenth-century politics. There have been many books on the Reform Bill campaign but without doubt the best is **Michael Brock**, *The Great Reform Act* (Hutchinson, 1973). Also useful on the issues raised in chapter 2 is the Historical Association pamphlet by **J.R. Dinwiddy**, *From Luddism to the First Reform Act* (Blackwell, 1986). For students seeking a more detailed analysis of the contribution of one radical to the movements of these years, **John Belchem**, *Orator Hunt: Henry Hunt and the English Working Class Radicalism* (Clarendon Press, 1985) is an admirable study in the tradition established by E.P. Thompson.

Working-class movements in the wake of the Reform Act are considered in **John Knott**, *Popular Opposition to the 1834 Poor Law* (Croom Helm, 1986), and **John Rule** (**ed**.), *British Trade Unionism 1750–1850: The Formative Years* (Longman, 1988).

Chartism has probably attracted more historians than any other single radical movement. The most recent narrative history is **J.T. Ward**, *Chartism* (Batsford, 1973). Ward takes the orthodox line on Chartism as a movement that wanted too much too soon and was betrayed by an inept leadership. A rather different approach is evident in **James Epstein**, *The Lion of Freedom* (Croom Helm, 1982), a biography of O'Connor. The best choice to extend the material on Chartism you have read is undoubtedly **Dorothy Thompson**, *The Chartists* (Temple Smith, 1984). A useful series of essays on various aspects of the movement is **J. Epstein and D. Thompson** (**eds**), *The Chartist Experience* (Macmillan, 1982). **Jutta Schwarzkopf**, *Women in the Chartist Movement* (Macmillan, 1991) provides a much needed study of the role that women played in the movement.

Coverage of working-class movements in the mid-Victorian period is rather more fragmentary. On the 1867 Reform Act two very different interpretations are presented in **Royden Harrison**, *Before the Socialists* (Macmillan, 1965) and **Maurice Cowling**, *1867: Disraeli, Gladstone, and Revolution* (Cambridge, 1967). The arguments are well summarised in, **J.K. Walton**, *The Second Reform Act* (Methuen, Lancaster Pamphlet 1987). The development of a new relationship between labour and capital, and the way this differed from their earlier relations during the Industrial Revolution, is explored in **Richard Price**, *Labour in British Society* (Croom Helm, 1986), chapters 1–4. A useful local study of this period, dealing with developments in Lancashire, is **Neville Kirk**, *The Growth of Working Class Reformism in Mid-Victorian England* (Groom Helm, 1985). There are also a number of helpful considerations of the 'labour aristocracy' available, particularly **Eric Hobsbawm**, *Worlds of Labour* (Wiedenfeld and Nicolson, 1984), chapters 13 and 14, and **Robert Gray**, *The Artistocracy of Labour in Nineteenth Century Britain* (Macmillan, 1981). This Economic History Society pamphlet presents a short, well reasoned, summary of the debate. **E.F. Biagini and A.J. Reid**, *Currents of Radicalism: Popular Radicalism, Organised Labour and Party Politics in Britain, 1850–1914* (CUP, 1991) presents a view of popular movements which stresses continuity and the diversity of working-class identities.

There is rather more material available on the rise of the Labour Party. See particularly, **Eric Hobsbawm**, *Labouring Men* (Wiedenfeld and Nicolson, 1964). This presents a series of essays on central themes, particularly in chapters 9–15. For a sensitive reconstruction of the energy of the socialist revival of the 1880s, in a way that is simply not available anywhere else, see **Stephen Yeo**, 'A new life: The religion of socialism in Britain, 1883–1896', *History Workshop Journal* (Autumn, 1977). On the Labour Party itself, two volumes of essays draw out important themes, **K. Laybourn and J. Reynolds**, *Liberalism and the Rise of Labour 1890–1918* (Croom Helm, 1984) (local studies of West Yorkshire) and **K.D. Brown** (**ed.**) *The First Labour Party 1906–1914* (Croom Helm, 1985); see particularly, Pat Thane's essay on the Labour Party's approach to social reform before the First World War. Thorough treatment of Labour in Parliament is to be found in **Ross McKibbin**, *The Evolution of the Labour Party 1910–1924* (OUP, 1974) and **D. Tanner**, *Political Change and the Labour Party 1900–1918* (Cambridge University Press, 1990). Biographical studies of the leading figures also provide a good way of understanding the difficulties Labour faced in these early years. Two good examples are **David Marquand**, *Ramsay MacDonald* (Cape, 1977), and **Iain Maclean**, *Keir Hardie* (Allen Lane, 1975).

Index